Elizabeth Price Sayer

Il Convito

The Banquet of Dante Alighieri

Elizabeth Price Sayer

Il Convito
The Banquet of Dante Alighieri

ISBN/EAN: 9783337188870

Printed in Europe, USA, Canada, Australia, Japan

Cover: Foto ©ninafisch / pixelio.de

More available books at **www.hansebooks.com**

THE BANQUET

OF

DANTE ALIGHIERI

TRANSLATED BY

ELIZABETH PRICE SAYER

WITH AN INTRODUCTION BY HENRY MORLEY
LL.D., PROFESSOR OF ENGLISH LITERATURE AT
UNIVERSITY COLLEGE, LONDON

LONDON
GEORGE ROUTLEDGE AND SONS
BROADWAY, LUDGATE HILL
GLASGOW AND NEW YORK
1887

MORLEY'S UNIVERSAL LIBRARY.

1. *Sheridan's Plays.*
2. *Plays from Molière.* By English Dramatists.
3. *Marlowe's Faustus* and *Goethe's Faust.*
4. *Chronicle of the Cid.*
5. *Rabelais' Gargantua* and the Heroic Deeds of *Pantagruel.*
6. *Machiavelli's Prince.*
7. *Bacon's Essays.*
8. *Defoe's Journal of the Plague Year.*
9. *Locke on Civil Government* and *Filmer's "Patriarcha."*
10. *Butler's Analogy of Religion.*
11. *Dryden's Virgil.*
12. *Scott's Demonology and Witchcraft.*
13. *Herrick's Hesperides.*
14. *Coleridge's Table-Talk.*
15. *Boccaccio's Decameron.*
16. *Sterne's Tristram Shandy.*
17. *Chapman's Homer's Iliad.*
18. *Mediæval Tales.*
19. *Voltaire's Candide,* and *Johnson's Rasselas.*
20. *Jonson's Plays and Poems.*
21. *Hobbes's Leviathan.*
22. *Samuel Butler's Hudibras.*
23. *Ideal Commonwealths.*
24. *Cavendish's Life of Wolsey.*
25 & 26. *Don Quixote.*
27. *Burlesque Plays and Poems.*
28. *Dante's Divine Comedy.* LONGFELLOW's Translation.
29. *Goldsmith's Vicar of Wakefield, Plays, and Poems.*
30. *Fables and Proverbs from the Sanskrit.* (*Hitopadesa.*)
31. *Lamb's Essays of Elia.*
32. *The History of Thomas Ellwood.*
33. *Emerson's Essays, &c.*
34. *Southey's Life of Nelson.*
35. *De Quincey's Confessions of an Opium-Eater, &c.*
36. *Stories of Ireland.* By Miss EDGEWORTH.
37. *Frere's Aristophanes: Acharnians, Knights, Birds.*
38. *Burke's Speeches and Letters.*
39. *Thomas à Kempis.*
40. *Popular Songs of Ireland.*
41. *Potter's Æschylus.*
42. *Goethe's Faust: Part II.* ANSTER's Translation.
43. *Famous Pamphlets.*
44. *Francklin's Sophocles.*
45. *M. G. Lewis's Tales of Terror and Wonder.*
46. *Vestiges of the Natural History of Creation.*
47. *Drayton's Barons' Wars, Nymphidia, &c.*
48. *Cobbett's Advice to Young Men.*
49. *Dante's Convito.*

"Marvels of clear type and general neatness."—*Daily Telegraph.*

INTRODUCTION.

THIS translation of Dante's Convito—the first in English—is from the hand of a lady whose enthusiasm for the genius of Dante has made it a chief pleasure of her life to dwell on it by translating, not his Divine Comedy only, but also the whole body of his other works. Among those works the Vita Nuova and the Convito have a distinct place, as leading up to the great masterpiece. In the New Life, Man starts on his career with human love that points to the divine. In the Banquet, he passes to mature life and to love of knowledge that declares the power and the love of God in the material and moral world about us and within us. In the Divine Comedy, the Poet passes to the world to come, and rises to the final union of the love for Beatrice, the beatifier, with the glory of the Love of God. Of this great series, the crowning work has, of course, had many translators, and there have been translators also of the book that shows the youth of love. But the noble fragment of the Convito that unites these two has, I believe, never yet been placed within reach of the English reader, except by a translation of its poems only into unrhymed measure in Mr. Charles Lyell's "Poems of the Vita Nuova and the Convito," published in 1835.

The Convito is a fragment. There are four books where fifteen were designed, including three only of the intended fourteen songs. But the plan is clear, and one or two glances forward to the matter of the last book, which would have had Justice for its theme, show that all was to have been brought to a high spiritual close.

Its aim was no less than the lifting of men's minds by knowledge of the world without them and within them, bound together in creation, showing forth the Mind of the Creator. The reader of this volume must not flinch from the ingenious dialectics of the mediæval reasoner on Man and Nature. Dante's knowledge is the knowledge of his time. Science had made little advance since Aristotle—who is "the Philosopher" taken by Dante for his human guide—first laid its foundations. It is useful, no doubt, to be able in a book like this, shaped by a noble mind, to study at their best the forms of reasoning that made the science of the Middle Ages. But the reader is not called upon to make his mind unhappy with endeavours to seize all the points, say, of a theory of the heavens that was most ingenious, but in no part true. The main thing is to observe how the mistaken reasoning joins each of the seven sciences to one of the seven heavens, and here as everywhere joins earth to heaven, and bids man lift his head and look up, Godward, to the source of light. If spiritual truth could only come from right and perfect knowledge, this would have been a world of dead souls from the first till now; for future centuries, in looking back at us, will wonder at the little faulty knowledge that we think so much. But let the known be what it may, the true soul rises from it to a sense of the divine mysteries of Wisdom and of Love. Dante's knowledge may be full of ignorance, and so is ours. But he fills it as he can with the Spirit of God. He is not content that men should be as sheep, and look downward to earth for all the food they need. He bids them to a Banquet of another kind, whose dishes are of knowledge for the mind and heavenward aspiration for the soul.

Dante's Convito—of which the name was, no doubt, suggested by the Banquets of Plato and Xenophon—was written at the close of his life, after the Divine Comedy, and no trace has been found of more of its songs than the three which may have been written and made known some time before he began work on their Commentary. Death stayed his hand, and the completion passed into a song that joined the voice of Dante to the praise in heaven.

H. M.

April 1887.

THE BANQUET OF DANTE ALIGHIERI.

The First Treatise.

CHAPTER I.

As the Philosopher says in the beginning of the first Philosophy: ["All men naturally desire Knowledge." The reason of which may be, that each thing, impelled by the intuition of its own nature, tends towards its perfection; hence, forasmuch as Knowledge is the final perfection of our Soul, in which our ultimate happiness consists, we are all naturally subject to the desire for it.]

Verily, many are deprived of this most noble perfection, by divers causes within the man and without him, which remove him from the use of Knowledge.

Within the man there may be two defects or impediments; the one on the part of the Body, the other on the part of the Soul. On the part of the Body it is, when the parts are unfitly disposed, so that it can receive nothing: as with the deaf and dumb, and their like. On the part of the Soul it is, when evil triumphs in it, so that it becomes the follower of vicious pleasures, through which it is so much deceived, that on account of them it holds everything in contempt.

Without the man, two causes may in like manner be understood, of which one comes of necessity, the other of stagnation. The first is the management of the family and conduct of civil affairs, which fitly draws to itself the greater number of men, so that they cannot live in the quietness of speculation. The other is the fault of the place where a person is born and reared, which will ofttimes be not only without any School whatever, but may be far distant from studious people. The two first of these causes—the first of the hindrance from within, and the first of the hindrance from without—are not deserving of blame, but of excuse and pardon; the two others, although the one more than the other, deserve blame and are to be detested.

Hence, he who reflects well, can manifestly see that they are few who can attain to the enjoyment of Knowledge, though it is desired by all, and almost innumerable are the fettered ones who live for ever famished of this food.

Oh, blessed are those few who sit at that table where the Bread of Angels is eaten, and wretched those who can feed only as the Sheep. But because each man is naturally friendly to each man, and each friend grieves for the fault of him whom he loves; they who are fed at that high table are full of mercy towards those whom they see straying in one pasture with the creatures who eat grass and acorns.

And forasmuch as Mercy is the Mother of Benevolence, those who know how, do always liberally offer their good wealth to the true poor, and are like a living stream, whose water cools the before-named natural thirst. I, then, who sit not at the blessed table, but having fled from the pasture of the common herd, lie at the feet of those who sit there and gather up what falls from them, by the sweetness which I find in that which I collect little by little, I know the wretched life of those whom I have left behind me ; and moved mercifully for the unhappy ones, not forgetting myself, I have reserved something which I have shown to their eyes long ago, and for this I have made them greatly desirous. Wherefore, now wishing to prepare for them, I mean to make a common Banquet of this which I have shown to them, and of that needed bread without which food such as this could not be eaten by them at their feast ; bread fit for such meat, which I know, without it, would be furnished forth in vain. And therefore I desire that no one should sit at this Banquet whose members are so unfitly disposed that he has neither teeth, nor tongue, nor palate : nor any follower of vice ; inasmuch as his stomach is full of venomous and hurtful humours, so that it will retain no food whatever. But let those come to us, whosoever they be, who, pressed by the management of civil and domestic life, have felt this human hunger, and at one table with others who have been in like bondage, let them sit. But at their feet let us place all those who have been the slaves of sloth, and who are not worthy to sit higher : and then let these and those eat of my dish, with the bread which I will cause them to taste and to digest.

The meat at this repast will be prepared in fourteen different ways, that is, in fourteen Songs, some of whose themes will be of Love and some of Virtue:

which, without the present bread, might have some shadow of obscurity, so that to many they might be acceptable more on account of their form than because of their spirit. But this bread is the present Exposition. It will be the Light whereby each colour of their design will be made visible.

And if in the present work, which is named "Convito"—the Banquet, the glad Life Together—I desire that the subject should be discussed more maturely than in the Vita Nuova—the New Life—I do not therefore mean in any degree to undervalue that Fresh Life, but greatly to enhance it; seeing how reasonable it is for that age to be fervid and passionate, and for this to be mature and temperate. At one age it is fit to speak and work in one way, and at another age in another way; because certain manners are fit and praiseworthy at one age which are improper and blameable at another, as will be demonstrated with suitable argument in the fourth treatise of this Book. In that first Book (Vita Nuova) at the entrance into my youth I spoke; and in this latter I speak after my youth has already passed away. And since my true meaning may be other than that which the aforesaid songs show forth, I mean by an allegoric exposition to explain these after the literal argument shall have been reasoned out: so that the one argument with the other shall give a relish to those who are the guests invited to this Banquet. And of them all I pray that if the feast be not so splendid as befits the proclamation thereof, let them impute each defect, not to my will but to my means, since my will here is to a full and loving Liberality.

CHAPTER II.

IN preparing for every well-ordered Banquet the servants are wont to take the proper bread, and see that it is clean from all blemish; wherefore I, who in the present writing stand in servant's place, intend firstly to remove two spots from this exposition which at my repast stands in the place of bread.

The one is, that it appears to be unlawful for any one to speak of himself; the other, that it seems to be unreasonable to speak too deeply when giving explanations. Let the knife of my judgment pare away from the present treatise the unlawful and the unreasonable. One does not permit any Rhetorician to speak of himself without a necessary cause. And from this is the man removed, because he can speak of no one without praise or blame of those of whom he speaks; which two causes commonly induce a man to speak of himself. And in order to remove a doubt which here arises, I say that it is worse for any one to blame than to praise himself, although neither may have to be done. The reason is, that anything which is essentially wrong is worse than that which is wrong through accident. For a man openly to bring contempt on himself is essentially wrong to his friend, because a man owes it to take account of his fault secretly, and no one is more friendly to himself than the man himself. In the chamber of his thoughts, therefore, he should reprove himself and weep over his faults, and not before the world. Again, a man is but seldom blamed when he has not the power or the knowledge requisite to guide himself aright: but he is always blamed when weak of will, because our good or evil dispositions are measured by the strength of will. Wherefore he who blames himself proves that he knows his fault, while he reveals his want of goodness; if, therefore, he know his fault, let him no more speak evil of himself. If a man praise himself it is to avoid evil, as it were; inasmuch as it cannot be done except such self-laudation become in excess dishonour; it is praise in appearance, it is infamy in substance. For the words are spoken to prove that of which he has not inward assurance. Hence, he who lauds himself proves his belief that he is not esteemed to be a good man, and this befalls him not unless he have an evil conscience, which he reveals by self-praise, and in so revealing it he blames himself.

And, again, self-praise and self-blame are to be shunned equally, for this reason, that it is false witnessing. Because there is no man who can be a true and just judge of himself, so much will self-love deceive him. Hence it happens that every man has in his own judgment the measures of the false merchant, who sells with the one, and buys with the other. Every man weights the scales against his own wrong-doing, and adds weight to his good deeds; so that the number and the quantity and the weight of the good deeds appear to him to be greater than if they were tried in a just balance; and in like manner the evil appears less. Wherefore speaking of himself with praise or with blame, either he speaks falsely with regard to the thing of which he speaks, or he speaks falsely by the fault of his judgment; and as the one is untruth, so is the other. And therefore, since to acquiesce is to admit, he is wrong who praises or who blames before the face of any man; because the man thus appraised can neither acquiesce nor deny without falling into the error of either praising or blaming himself. Reserve the way of due correction, which cannot be taken without reproof of error, and which corrects if understood. Reserve also the way of due honour and glory, which cannot be taken without mention of virtuous works, or of dignities that have been worthily acquired.

And in truth, returning to the main argument, I say, as before, that it is permitted to a man for requisite reasons to speak of himself. And amongst the several requisite reasons two are most evident: the one is when a man cannot avoid great danger and infamy, unless he discourse of himself; and then it is conceded for the reason, that to take the less objectionable of the only two paths, is to take as it were a good one. And this necessity moved Boethius to speak of himself, in order that under pretext of Consolation he might excuse the perpetual shame of his imprisonment, by showing that imprisonment to be unjust; since no other man arose to justify him. And this reason moved St. Augustine to speak of himself in his Confessions; that, by the progress of his life, which was from bad to good, and from good to better, and from better to best, he might give example and instruction, which, from truer testimony, no one could receive. Therefore, if either of these reasons excuse me, the bread of my moulding is sufficiently cleared from its first impurity.

The fear of shame moves me; and I am moved by the desire to give instruction which others truly are unable to give. I fear shame for having followed passion so ardently, as he may conceive who reads the afore-named Songs, and sees how greatly I was ruled by it; which shame ceases entirely by the present speech of myself, which proves that not passion but virtue may have been the moving cause.

I intend also to demonstrate the true meaning of those Poems, which some could not perceive unless I relate it, because it is concealed under the veil of Allegory; and this it not only will give pleasure to hear, but subtle instruction, both as to the diction and as to the intention of the other writings

CHAPTER III.

MUCH fault is in that thing which is appointed to remove some grave evil, and yet encourages it; even as in the man who might be sent to quell a tumult, and, before he had quelled it, should begin another.

And forasmuch as my bread is made clean on one side, it behoves me to cleanse it on the other, in order to shun this reproof: that my writing, which one may term, as it were, a Commentary, is appointed to remove obscurity from the before-mentioned Songs, and is, in fact, itself at times a little hard to understand. This obscurity is here intended, in order to avoid a greater defect, and does not occur through ignorance. Alas! would that it might have pleased the Dispenser of the Universe that the cause of my excuse might never have been; that others might neither have sinned against me, nor I have suffered punishment unjustly; the punishment, I say, of exile and poverty! Since it was the pleasure of the citizens of the most beautiful and the most famous daughter of Rome, Florence, to cast me out from her most sweet bosom (wherein I was born and nourished even to the height of my life, and in which, with her goodwill, I desire with all my heart to repose my weary soul, and to end the time which is given to me), I have gone through almost all the land in which this language lives—a pilgrim, almost a mendicant—showing forth against my will the wound of Fortune, with which the ruined man is often unjustly reproached. Truly I have been a ship without a sail and without a rudder, borne to divers ports and lands and shores by the dry wind which blows from doleful poverty; and I have appeared vile in the eyes of many, who perhaps through some report may have imaged me in other form. In the sight of whom not only my person became vile, but each work already completed was held to be of less value than that might again be which remained yet to be done.

The reason wherefore this happens (not only to me but to all), it now pleases me here briefly to touch upon. And firstly, it is because rumour goes beyond the truth; and then, what is beyond the truth restricts and strangles it. Good report is the first-born of kindly thought in the mind of the friend; which the mind of the foe, although it may receive the seed, conceives not.

That mind which gives birth to it in the first place, so to make its gift more fair, as by the charity of friendship, keeps not within bounds of truth, but passes beyond them. When one does that to adorn a tale, he speaks against his conscience; when it is charity that causes him to pass the bounds, he speaks not against conscience.

The second mind which receives this, not only is content with the exaggeration of the first mind, but its own report adds its own effect of endeavours to embellish, and so by this action, and by the deception which it also receives from the goodwill generated in it, good report is made more ample than it should be; either with the consent or the dissent of the conscience; even as it was with the first mind. And the third receiving mind does this; and the fourth; and thus the exaggeration of good ever grows. And so, by turning the aforesaid motives in the contrary direction, one can perceive why ill-fame in like manner is made to grow. Wherefore Virgil says in the fourth of the Æneid: "Let Fame live to be fickle, and grow as she goes." Clearly, then, he who is willing may perceive that the image generated by Fame alone is always larger, whatever it may be, than the thing imaged is, in its true state.

CHAPTER IV.

HAVING previously shown the reason why Fame magnifies the good and the evil beyond due limit, it remains in this chapter to show forth those reasons which make evident why the Presence restricts in the opposite way, and having shown this I will return to the principal proposition. I say, then, that for three causes his Presence makes a person of less value than he is. The first is childishness, I do not say of age, but of mind; the second is envy; and these are in the judge: the third is human impurity; and this is in the person judged. The first, one can briefly reason thus: the greater part of men live according to sense and not according to reason, after the manner of children, and the like of these judge things simply from without; and the goodness which is ordained to a fit end they perceive not, because the eyes of Reason, which they need in order to perceive it, are closed. Hence, they soon see all that they can, and judge according to their sight.

And forasmuch as any opinion they form on the good fame of others, from hearsay, with which, in the presence of the person judged, their imperfect judgment may dissent, they amend not according to reason, because they judge merely according to sense, they will deem that which they have first heard to be a lie as it were, and dispraise the person who was previously praised. Hence, in such men, and such are almost all, Presence restricts the one fame and the other. Such men as these are inconstant and are soon cloyed; they are often gay and often sad from brief joys and sorrows; speedy friends and speedy foes; each thing they do like children, without the use of reason.

The second observation from these reasons is, that due comparison is cause for envy to the vicious; and envy is a cause of evil judgment, because it does not permit Reason to argue for that which is envied, and the judicial power is then like the judge who hears only one side. Hence, when such men as these perceive a person to be famous, they are immediately jealous, because they compare members and powers; and they fear, on account of the excellence of such an one, to be themselves accounted of less worth; and these passionate men, not only judge evilly, but, by defamation, they cause others to judge evilly. Wherefore with such men their apprehension restricts the acknowledgment of good and evil in each person represented; and I say this also of evil, because many who delight in evil deeds have envy towards evil-doers.

The third observation is of human frailty, which

one accepts on the part of him who is judged, and from which familiar conversation is not altogether free. In evidence of this, it is to be known that man is stained in many parts; and, as says St. Augustine, "none is without spot." Now, the man is stained with some passion, which he cannot always resist; now, he is blemished by some fault of limb; now, he is bruised by some blow from Fortune; now, he is soiled by the ill-fame of his parents, or of some near relation: things which Fame does not bear with her, but which hang to the man, so that he reveals them by his conversation; and these spots cast some shadow upon the brightness of goodness, so that they cause it to appear less bright and less excellent. And this is the reason why each prophet is less honoured in his own country; and this is why the good man ought to give his presence to few, and his familiarity to still fewer, in order that his name may be received and not despised. And this third observation may be the same for the evil as for the good, if we reverse the conditions of the argument. Wherefore it is clearly evident that by imperfections, from which no one is free, the seen Presence restricts right perception of the good and of the evil in every one, more than truth desires. Hence, since, as has been said above, I myself have been, as it were, visibly present to all the Italians, by which I perhaps am made more vile than truth desires, not only to those to whom my repute had already run, but also to others, whereby I am made the lighter; it behoves me that with a more lofty style I may give to the present work a little gravity, through which it may show greater authority. Let this suffice to excuse the difficulty of my commentary.

CHAPTER V.

SINCE this bread is now cleared of accidental spots, it remains to excuse it from a substantial one, that is for being in my native tongue and not in Latin; which by similitude one may term, of barley-meal and not of wheaten flour. And from this it is briefly excused by three reasons which moved me to choose the one rather than the other. One springs from the avoidance of inconvenient Unfitness: the second from the readiness of well-adjusted Liberality; the third from the natural Love for one's own Native Tongue. And these things, with the grounds for them, to the staying of all possible reproof, I mean in due order to reason out in this form.

That which most adorns and commends human actions, and which most directly leads them to a good result, is the use of dispositions best adapted to the end in view; as the end aimed at in knighthood is courage of mind and strength of body. And thus he who is ordained to the service of others, ought to have those dispositions which are suited to that end; as submission, knowledge and obedience, without which any one is unfit to serve well. Because if he is not subject to each of these conditions, he proceeds in his service always with fatigue and trouble, and but seldom continues in it. If he is not obedient, he never serves except as in his wisdom he thinks fit, and when he wills; which is rather the service of a friend than of a servant. Hence, to escape this disorder, this commentary is fit, which is made as a servant to the under-written Songs, in order to be subject to these, and to each separate command of theirs. It must be conscious of the wants of its lord, and obedient to him; which dispositions would be all wanting to it if it were a Latin servant, not a native, since the songs are all in the language of our people. For, in the first place, if it had been a Latin servant he would be not a subject but a sovereign, in nobility, in virtue, and in beauty; in nobility, because the Latin is perpetual and incorruptible; the language of the vulgar is unstable and corruptible. Hence we see in the ancient writings of the Latin Comedies and Tragedies that they cannot change, being the same Latin that we now have; this happens not with our native tongue, which, being home-made, changes at pleasure. Hence we see in the cities of Italy, if we will look carefully back fifty years from the present time, many words to have become extinct, and to have been born, and to have been altered. But if a little time transforms them thus, a longer time changes them more. So that I say that, if those who departed from this life a thousand years ago should come back to their cities, they would believe those cities to be inhabited by a strange people, who speak a tongue discordant from their own. On this subject I will speak elsewhere more completely in a book which I intend to write, God willing, on the "Language of the People."

Again, the Latin was not subject, but sovereign, through virtue. Each thing has virtue in its nature, which does that to which it is ordained; and the better it does it so much the more virtue it has: hence we call that man virtuous who lives a life contemplative or active, doing that for which he is best fitted; we ascribe his virtue to the horse that runs swiftly and much, to which end he is ordained: we see virtue of a sword that cuts through hard things well, since it has been made to do so. Thus speech, which is ordained to express human thought, has virtue when it does that; and most virtue is in the speech which does it most. Hence, forasmuch as the Latin reveals many things conceived in the mind which the vulgar tongue cannot express, even as those know who have the use of either language, its virtue is far greater than that of the vulgar tongue.

Again, it was not subject, but sovereign, because of its beauty. That thing man calls beautiful whose parts are duly proportionate, because beauty results from their harmony; hence, man appears to be beautiful when his limbs are duly proportioned; and we call a song beautiful when the voices in it, according to the rule of art, are in harmony with each other. Hence, that language is most beautiful in which the words most fitly correspond, and this they do more in the Latin than in the present Language of the People, since the beautiful vulgar tongue follows use, and the Latin, Art. Hence, one concedes it to be more beautiful, more virtuous and more noble. And so one concludes, as first proposed; that is, that the Latin Commentary would have been the Sovereign, not the Subject, of the Songs.

CHAPTER VI.

HAVING shown how the present Commentary could not have been the subject of Songs written in our native tongue, if it had been in the Latin, it remains to show how it could not have been capable or obedient to those Songs; and then it will be shown how, to avoid unsuitable disorder, it was needful to speak in the native tongue.

I say that Latin would not have been a capable servant for my Lord the Vernacular, for this reason. The servant is required chiefly to know two things perfectly: the one is the nature of his lord, because there are lords of such an asinine nature that they command the opposite of that which they desire; and there are others who, without speaking, wish to be understood and served; and there are others who will not let the servant move to do that which is needful, unless they have ordered it. And because these variations are in men, I do not intend in the present work to show, for the digression would be enlarged too much, except as I speak in general, that such men as these are beasts, as it were, to whom reason is of little worth. Wherefore, if the servant know not the nature of his lord, it is evident that he cannot serve him perfectly. The other thing is, that it is requisite for the servant to know also the friends of his lord; for otherwise he could not honour them, nor serve them, and thus he would not serve his lord perfectly: forasmuch as the friends are the parts of a whole, as it were, because their whole is one wish or its opposite. Neither would the Latin Commentary have had such knowledge of those things as the vulgar tongue itself has. That the Latin cannot be acquainted with the Vulgar Tongue and with its friends, is thus proved. He who knows anything in general knows not that thing perfectly; even as he who knows from afar off one animal, knows not that animal perfectly, because he knows not if it be a dog, a wolf, or a he-goat. The Latin knows the Vulgar tongue in general, but not separately; for if it should know it separately it would know all the Vulgar Tongues, because it is not right that it should know one more than the other ; and thus, what man soever might possess the complete knowledge of the Latin tongue, the use of that knowledge would show him all distinctions of the Vulgar. But this is not so, for one used to the Latin does not distinguish, if he be a native of Italy, the vulgar tongue of Provence from the German, nor can the German distinguish the vulgar Italian tongue from that of Provence : hence, it is evident that the Latin is not cognizant of the Vulgar. Again, it is not cognizant of its friends, because it is impossible to know the friends without knowing the principal ; hence, if the Latin does not know the Vulgar, as it is proved above, it is impossible for it to know its friends. Again, without conversation or familiarity, it is impossible to know men ; and the Latin has no conversation with so many in any language as the Vulgar has, to which all are friends, and consequently cannot know the friends of the Vulgar.

And this, that it would be possible to say, is no contradiction ; that the Latin does converse with some friends of the Vulgar : but since it is not familiar with all, it is not perfectly acquainted with its friends, whereas perfect knowledge is required, and not defective.

CHAPTER VII.

HAVING proved that the Latin Commentary could not have been a capable servant, I will tell how it could not have been an obedient one. He is obedient who has the good disposition which is called obedience. True obedience must have three things, without which it cannot be: it should be sweet, and not bitter; entirely under control, and not impulsive; with due measure, and not excessive; which three things it was impossible for the Latin Commentary to have; and, therefore, it was impossible for it to be obedient. That to the Latin it would have been impossible, as is said, is evident by such an argument as this: each thing which proceeds by an inverse order is laborious, and consequently is bitter, and not sweet; even as to sleep by day and to wake by night, and to go backwards and not forwards. For the subject to command the sovereign, is to proceed in the inverse order; because the direct order is, for the sovereign to command the subject; and thus it is bitter, and not sweet; and because to the bitter command it is impossible to give sweet obedience, it is impossible, when the subject commands, for the obedience of the sovereign to be sweet. Hence if the Latin is the sovereign of the Vulgar Tongue, as is shown above by many reasons, and the Songs, which are in place of commanders, are in the Vulgar Tongue, it is impossible for the argument to be sweet. Then is obedience entirely commanded, and in no way spontaneous, when that which the obedient man does, he would not have done of his own will, either in whole or in part, without commandment. And, therefore, if it might be commanded to me to carry two long robes upon my back, and if without commandment I should carry one, I say that my obedience is not entirely commanded, but is in part spontaneous; and such would have been that of the Latin Commentary, and consequently it would not have been obedience entirely commanded. What such might have been appears by this, that the Latin, without the command of this Lord, the Vernacular, would have expounded many parts of his argument (and it does expound, as he who searches well the books written in Latin may perceive), which the Vulgar Tongue does nowhere.

Again, obedience is within bounds, and not excessive, when it goes to the limit of the command, and no further; as Individual Nature is obedient to Universal Nature when she makes thirty-two teeth in the man, and no more and no less; and when she makes five fingers on the hand, and no more and no less; and the man is obedient to Justice when he does that which the Law commands, and no more and no less.

Neither would the Latin have done this, but it would have sinned not only in the defect, and not only in the excess, but in each one; and thus its obedience would not have been within due limit, but intemperate, and consequently it would not have been obedient. That the Latin would not have been the executor of the commandment of his Lord, and that neither would he have been a usurper, one can easily prove. This Lord, namely, these Songs, to which this Commentary is ordained for their servant, commands and desires that they shall be explained to all those whose mind is so far intelligent that when they hear speech they can understand, and when they speak they can be understood. And no one doubts, that if the Songs should command by word of mouth, this would be their commandment. But the Latin would not have explained them, except to the learned men: and so that the rest could not have understood. Hence, forasmuch as the number of unlearned men who desire to understand those Songs may be far greater than the learned, it follows that it could not have fulfilled its commandment so well as the Native Tongue, which is understood both by the Learned and the Unlearned. Again, the Latin would have explained them to people of another language, as to the Germans, to the English, and to others; and here it would have exceeded their commandment. For against their will, speaking freely, I say, their meaning would be explained there where they could not convey it in all their beauty.

And, therefore, let each one know, that nothing which is harmonized by the bond of the Muse can be translated from its own language into another, without breaking all its sweetness and harmony. And this is the reason why Homer was not translated from Greek into Latin, like the other writings that we have of the Greeks. And this is the reason why the verses of the Psalms are without sweetness of music and harmony; for they were translated from Hebrew into Greek, and from Greek into Latin, and in the first translation all that sweetness vanished.

And, thus is concluded that which was proposed in the beginning of the chapter immediately before this.

CHAPTER VIII.

SINCE it is proved by sufficient reasons that, in order to avoid unsuitable confusion, it would be right that the above-named Songs be opened and explained by a Commentary in our Native Tongue and not in the Latin, I intend to show again how a ready Liberality makes me select this way and leave the other. It is possible, then, to perceive a ready Liberality in three things, which go with this Native Tongue, and which would not have gone with the Latin. The first is to give to many; the second is to give useful things; the third is to give the gift without being asked for it.

For to give to and to assist one person is good; but to give to and to assist many is ready goodness, inasmuch as it has a similitude to the good gifts of God, who is the Benefactor of the Universe. And again, to give to many is impossible without giving to one, forasmuch as one is included in many. But to give to one may be good without giving to many, because he who assists many does good to one and to the other; he who assists one does good to one only: hence, we see the imposers of the laws, especially if they are for the common good, hold the eyes fixed whilst compiling these laws. Again, to give useless things to the receiver is also a good, inasmuch as he who gives, shows himself at least to be a friend; but it is not a perfect good, and therefore it is not ready: as if a knight should give to a doctor a shield, and as if the doctor should give to a knight the written aphorisms of Hippocrates, or rather the technics of Galen; because the wise men say that "the face of the gift ought to be similar to that of the receiver,".that is, that it be suitable to him, and that it be useful; and therein it is called ready liberality in him who thus discriminates in giving.

But forasmuch as moral discourses usually create a desire to see their origin, in this chapter I intend briefly to demonstrate four reasons why of necessity the gift (in order that it be ready liberality) should be useful to him who receives. Firstly, because virtue must be cheerful and not sad in every action: hence, if the gift be not cheerful in the giving and in the receiving, in it there is not perfect nor ready virtue. And this joy can spring only from the utility, which resides in the giver through the giving, and which comes to the receiver through the receiving. In the giver, then, there must be the foresight, in doing this, that on his part there shall remain the benefit of an inherent virtue which is above all other advantages; and that to the receiver come the benefit of the use of the thing given. Thus the one and the other will be cheerful, and consequently it will be a ready liberality, that is, a liberality both prompt and well considered.

Secondly, because virtue ought always to move things forwards and upwards. For even as it would be a blameable action to make a spade of a beautiful sword, or to make a fair basin of a lovely lute; so it is wrong to move anything from a place where it may be useful, and to carry it into a place where it may be less useful. And since it is blameable to work in vain, it is wrong not merely to put the thing in a place where it may be less useful, but even in a place where it may be equally useful. Hence, in order that the changing of the place of a thing may be laudable, it must always be for the better, because it ought to be especially praiseworthy; and this the gift cannot be, if by transformation it become not more precious. Nor can it become more precious, if it be not more useful to the receiver than to the giver. Wherefore, one concludes that the gift must be useful to him who receives it, in order that it may be in itself ready liberality.

Thirdly, because the exercise of the virtue of itself ought to be the acquirer of friends. For our life has need of these, and the end of virtue is to make life happy. But that the gift may make the receiver a friend, it must be useful to him, because utility stamps on the memory the image of the gift, which is the food of friendship, and the firmer the impression, so much the greater is the utility; hence, Martino was wont to say, "Never will fade from my mind the gift Giovanni made me." Wherefore, in order that in the gift there may be its virtue, which is Liberality, and that it may be ready, it must be useful to him who receives it.

Finally, since the act of virtue should be free, not forced, it is free action, when a person goes willingly to any place; which is shown by his keeping the face turned thitherward; it is forced action, when he goes against his will; which is shown by his not looking cheerfully towards the place whither he goes: and thus the gift looks towards its appointed place when it addresses itself to the need of the receiver. And since it cannot address itself to that need except it be useful, it follows, in order that it may be with free action, that the virtue be free, and that the gift go freely to its object, which is the receiver; and consequently the gift must be to the utility of the receiver, in order that there may be a prompt and reasonable Liberality therein.

The third respect in which one can observe a ready Liberality, is giving unasked; because, to give what is asked, is, on one side, not virtue, but traffic; for, the receiver buys, although the giver may not sell; and so Seneca says "that nothing is purchased more dearly than that whereon prayers are expended." Hence, in order that in the gift there be ready Liberality, and that one may perceive that to be in it, there must be freedom from each act of traffic, and the gift must be unasked. Wherefore that which is besought costs us so dear, I do not mean to argue now, because it will be fully discussed in the last treatise of this book.

CHAPTER IX.

A LATIN Commentary would be wanting in all the three above-mentioned conditions, which must concur, in order that in the benefit conferred there may be ready Liberality; and our Mother Tongue possesses all, as it is possible to show thus manifestly. The Latin would not have served many; for if we recall to memory that which is discoursed of above, the learned men, without the Italian tongue, could not have had this service. And those who know Latin, if we wish to see clearly who they are, we shall find that, out of a thousand one only would have been reasonably served by it, because they would not have received it, so prompt are they to avarice, which removes them from each nobility of soul that especially desires this food. And to the shame of them, I say that they ought not to be called learned men: because they do not acquire knowledge for the use of it, but forasmuch as they gain money or dignity thereby; even as one ought not to call him a harper who keeps a harp in his house to be lent out for a price, and not to use it for its music.

Returning, then, to the principal proposition, I say that one can see clearly how the Latin would have given its good gift to few, but the Mother Tongue will serve many. For the willingness of heart which awaits this service, is in those who, through misuse of the world, have left Literature to men who have made of her a harlot; and these nobles are princes, barons, knights, and many other noble people, not only men, but women, whose language is that of the people and unlearned. Again, the Latin would not have been giver of a

I was moved in the first place to exalt it. And that I do exalt it may be seen by this reason: it happens that it is possible to magnify things in many conditions of greatness, and nothing makes so great as the greatness of that goodness which is the mother and preserver of all other forms of greatness. And no greater goodness can a man have than that of virtuous action, which is his own goodness, by which the greatness of true dignity and of true honour, of true power, of true riches, of true friends, of true and pure renown, are acquired and preserved: and this greatness I give to this friend, inasmuch as that which he had of goodness in latent power and hidden, I cause him to have in action and revealed in its own operation, which is to declare thought.

Secondly, I was moved by jealousy of it. The jealousy of the friend makes a man anxious to secure lasting provision; wherefore, thinking that, from the desire to understand these Songs, some unlearned man would have translated the Latin Commentary into the Mother Tongue; and fearing that the Mother Tongue might have been employed by some one who would have made it seem ugly, as he did who translated the Latin of the "Ethics," I endeavoured to employ it, trusting in myself more than in any other. Again, I was moved to defend it from its numerous accusers, who depreciate it and commend others, especially the Langue d'Oc, saying, that the latter is more beautiful and better than this, therein deviating from the truth. For by this Commentary the great excellence of our common Lingua di Sì will appear, since (through it, most lofty and most original ideas may be as fitly, sufficiently, and easily expressed as if it were by the Latin itself, which cannot show its virtue in things rhymed because of accidental ornaments which are connected therewith—that is, the rhyme and the rhythm, or the regulated measure; as it is with the beauty of a lady when the splendour of the jewels and of the garments excite more admiration than she herself. He, therefore, who wishes to judge well of a lady looks at her when she is alone and her natural beauty is with her, free from all accidental ornament. So it will be with this Commentary, in which will be seen the facility of the syllables, the propriety of the conditions, and the sweet orations which are made in our Mother Tongue, which a good observer will perceive to be full of most sweet and most amiable beauty. But, since it is most determined in its intention to show the error and the malice of the accuser, I will tell, to the confusion of those who accuse the Italian language, wherefore they are moved to do this; and this I shall do in a special chapter, in order that their shame may be more notable.

CHAPTER XI.

To the perpetual shame and abasement of the evil men of Italy who commend the Mother Tongue of other nations and depreciate their own, I say that their action proceeds from five abominable causes: the first is blindness of discretion; the second, mischievous self-justification; the third, greed of vainglory; the fourth, an invention of envy; the fifth and last, vileness of mind, that is, cowardice. And each one of these grave faults has a great following, for few are those who are free from them.

Of the first, one can reason thus. As the sensitive part of the soul has its eyes, with which it learns the difference of things, inasmuch as they are coloured externally; so the rational part has its eye with which it learns the difference of things, inasmuch as each is ordained to some end; and this is discretion. And as he who is blind with the eyes of sense goes always according to the guidance of others judging evil and good; so he who is blinded from the light of discretion, always goes in his judgment according to the cry, right or wrong as it may be. Hence, whenever the guide is blind, it must follow that what blind man soever leans on him must come to a bad end. Therefore it is written that, "If the blind lead the blind, both fall into the ditch." This cry has been long raised against our Mother Tongue, for the reasons which will be argued below.

After this cry the blind men above mentioned, who are infinite, as it were with one hand on the shoulder of these false witnesses, have fallen into the ditch of false opinion, from which they know not how to escape. From the use of the sight of discretion the mass of the people are debarred, because each being occupied from the early years of his life with some trade, he so directs his mind to that, by force of necessity, that he understands nought else. And forasmuch as the habit of virtue, moral as well as intellectual, cannot possibly be had all on a sudden, but it must be acquired through long custom, and as these people place their custom in some art, and care not to discern other things, it is impossible to them to have discretion. Wherefore it happens that often they cry aloud: "Long live Death!" and "Let Life die!" because some one begins the cry. And this is the most dangerous defect in their blindness. For this reason Boethius judges glory of the people vain, because he sees it to be without discernment. These persons are to be termed sheep and not men; for if a sheep should leap over a precipice of a thousand feet, all the others would follow after it; and if one sheep, for some cause or other, in crossing a road, leaps, all the others leap, even when they see nothing to leap over. And I once saw many leap into a well, because one had leapt into it, believing perhaps that it was leaping a wall; notwithstanding that the shepherd, weeping and shouting, with arms and breast set himself against them.

The second faction against our Mother Tongue springs from a malicious self-justification. There are many who would rather be thought masters than be such; and to avoid the opposite—that is, to be held not to be such—they always cast blame on the material they work on, or upon the instrument; as the clumsy smith blames the iron given to him, and the bad harpist blames the harp, thinking to cast the blame of the bad blade and of the bad music upon the iron and upon the harp, and to lift it from themselves. Thus there are some, and not a few, who desire that a man may hold them to be orators; and to excuse themselves for not speaking, or for speaking badly, they accuse or throw blame on the material, that is, their own Mother Tongue, and praise that of other lands, which they are not required to employ. And he who wishes to see wherefore this iron is to be blamed, let him look at the work which good artificers make of it, and he will understand the malice of those who, in casting blame upon it, think thereby to excuse themselves.

Against such as these, Tullius exclaims in the beginning of his book, which he names the book "De Finibus," because in his time they blamed the Roman Latin, and praised the Greek grammar. And thus I say, for like reasons, that these men vilify the Italian tongue, and glorify that of Provence.

The third faction against our Mother Tongue springs from greed of vainglory. There are many who, by describing certain things in some other language, and by praising that language, deem themselves to be more worthy of admiration than if they described them in their own. And undoubtedly to learn well a foreign tongue is deserving of some praise for intellect; but it is a blameable thing to applaud that language beyond truth, to glorify one's self for such an acquisition.

The fourth springs from an invention of envy. So that, as it is said above, envy is always where there is equality. Amongst the men of one nation there is the equality of the native tongue; and because one knows not how to use it like the other, therefrom springs envy. The envious man then argues, not blaming himself for not knowing how to speak like him who does speak as he should, but he blames that which is the material of his work, in order to rob, by depreciating the work on that side, him who does speak, of honour and fame; like him who should find fault with the blade of a sword, not in order to throw blame on the sword, but on the whole work of the master.

The fifth and last faction springs from vileness of mind. The magnanimous man always praises himself in his heart; and so the pusillanimous man, on the contrary, always deems himself less than he is. And because to magnify and to diminish always have respect to something, by comparison with which the large-minded man makes himself great and the small-minded man makes himself small, it results therefrom that the magnanimous man always makes others less than they are, and the pusillanimous makes others always greater. And therefore with that measure wherewith a man measures himself, he measures his own things, which are as it were a part of himself. It results that to the magnanimous man his own things always appear better than they are, and those of others less good; the pusillanimous man always believes his things to be of little value, and those of others of much worth. Wherefore many, on account of this vileness of mind, depreciate their native tongue, and applaud that of others; and all such as these are the abominable wicked men of Italy who hold this precious Mother Tongue in vile contempt, which if it be vile in any case, is so only inasmuch as it sounds in the evil mouth of these adulterers, under whose guidance go those blind men of whom I spoke in the first argument.

CHAPTER XII.

IF flames of fire should issue visibly through the windows of a house, and if any one should ask if there were fire within it, and if another should answer "Yes" to him, one would not well know how to judge which of those might be mocking the most. Not otherwise would the question and the answer pass between me and that man who should ask me if love for my own language is in me, and if I should answer "Yes" to him, after the arguments propounded above.

But, nevertheless, it has to be proved that not only love, but the most perfect love for it exists in me, and again its adversaries must be blamed. Whilst demonstrating this to him who will understand well, I will tell how I became the friend of it, and then how my friendship is confirmed.

I say that (as Tullius writes in his book on Friendship, not dissenting from the opinion of the Philosopher opened up in the eighth and in the ninth of the Ethics) Neighbourhood and Goodness are, naturally, the causes of the birth of Love: Benevolence, Study, and Custom are the causes of the growth of Love. And there have been all these causes to produce and to strengthen the love which I bear to my Native Language, as I shall briefly demonstrate. A thing is so much the nearer in proportion as it is most nearly allied to all the other things of its own kind; wherefore, of all men the son is nearest to the father, and of all the Arts, Medicine is nearest to the Doctor, and Music to the Musician, because they are more allied to them than the others. Of all parts of the earth the nearest is that whereon a man lives, because he is most united to it. And thus his own Native Language is nearest to him, inasmuch as he is most united to it; for it, and it alone, is first in the mind before any other. And not only of itself is it united, but by accident, inasmuch as it is united with the persons nearest to him, as his parents, and his fellow-citizens, and his own people. And this is his own Mother Tongue, which is not only nearest, but especially the nearest to each man. Therefore, if near neighbourhood be the seed of friendship, as is said above, it is manifest that it has been one of the causes of the love which I bear to my Native Language, which is nearer to me than the others. The above-mentioned cause, whereby that alone which stands first in each mind is most bound to it, gave rise to the custom of the people, that the first-born sons should succeed to the inheritance solely as being the nearest relatives; and because the nearest relatives, therefore the most beloved.

Again, Goodness made me a friend to it. And here it is to be known that all goodness inherent in anything is loveable in that thing; as in manhood to be well bearded, and in womanhood to be all over the face quite free from hair; as in the setter to have good scent, and as in the greyhound to be swift. And in proportion as it is native, so much the more is it delightful. Hence, although each virtue is loveable in man, that is the most loveable in him which is most human: and this is Justice, which alone is in the rational part, or rather in the intellectual, that is, in the Will. This is so loveable that as says the Philosopher in the fifth book of the Ethics, its enemies love it, such as thieves and robbers; and, therefore, we see that its opposite, that is, Injustice, is especially hated; such as treachery, ingratitude, falsehood, theft, rapine, deceit, and their like; the which are such inhuman sins, that, in order to excuse himself from the infamy of such, it is granted through long custom that a man may speak of himself, as has been said above, and may say if he be faithful and loyal. Of this virtue I shall speak hereafter more fully in the fourteenth treatise; and here quitting it, I return to the proposition. Having proved, then, that the goodness of a thing is loved the more the more it is innate, the more it is to be loved and commended for itself, it remains to see what that goodness is. And we see that, in all speech, to express a thought well and clearly is the thing most to be admired and commended. This, then, is its first goodness. And forasmuch as this is in our Mother Tongue, as is made evident in another chapter, it is manifest that it has been the cause of the love which I bear to it; since, as has been said, "Goodness is the producer of Love."

CHAPTER XIII.

HAVING said how in the Mother Tongue there are those two things which have made me its friend, that is, nearness to me and its innate goodness, I will tell how by kindness and union in study, and through the benevolence of long use, the friendship is confirmed and grows. Firstly, I say that I for myself have received from it the greatest benefits. And, therefore, it is to be known that, amongst all benefits, that is the greatest which is most precious to him who receives it; and nothing is so precious as that through which all other things are wished; and all the other things are wished for the perfection of him who wishes. Wherefore, inasmuch as a man may have two perfections, one first and one second (the first causes him to be, the second causes him to be good), if the Native Language has been to me the cause of the one and of the other, I have received from it the greatest benefit. And that it may have been the cause of this condition in me can be shown briefly. The efficient cause for the existence of things is not one only, but among many efficient causes one is the chief of the others, hence the fire and the hammer are the efficient causes of the sword-blade, although the workman is especially so. This my Mother Tongue was the bond of union between my forefathers, who spoke with it, even as the fire is the link between the iron and the smith who makes the knife; therefore it is evident that it co-operated in my birth, and so it was in some way the cause of my being. Again, this my Mother Tongue was my introducer into the path of knowledge, which is the ultimate perfection, inasmuch as with it I entered into the Latin Language, and with it I was taught; the which Latin was then the way of further advancement for me. And so it is evident and known by me that this my language has been my great benefactor. Also it has been engaged with me in one self-same study, and this I can thus prove. Each thing naturally studies its self-preservation; hence, if the Mother Tongue could seek anything of itself, it would seek that; and that would be to secure for itself a position of the greatest stability: but greater stability it could not secure than by uniting itself with number and with rhyme.

And this self-same study has been mine, as is so evident that it requires no testimony; therefore its study and mine have been one and the same, whereby the harmony of friendship is confirmed and increased. Also between us there has been the benevolence of long use: for from the beginning of my life I have had with it kind fellowship and conversation, and have used it, when deliberating, interpreting, and questioning; wherefore, if friendship increases through long use, as in all reason appears, it is manifest that in me it has increased especially, for with this my Mother Tongue I have spent all my time. And thus one sees that to the shaping of this friendship there have co-operated all causes of birth and growth. Therefore, let it be concluded that not only Love, but the most Perfect Love, is that which I have for it. So it is, and ought to be.

Thus, casting the eyes backwards and gathering up the afore-stated reasons, one can see that this Bread, with which the Meat of the under-written Poems ought to be eaten, is made clear enough of blemishes, and of fault in the nature of its grain. Wherefore, it is time to attend to and serve up the viands.

This will be that barley-bread with which a thousand will satisfy themselves; and my full baskets shall overflow with it. This will be that new Light, that new Sun, which shall rise when the sun of this our day shall set, and shall give light to those who are in darkness and in gloom because the sun of this our day gives light to them no more.

The Second Treatise.

Ye who the third Heaven move, intent of thought,
   Hear reasoning that is within my heart,
   Thoughts that to none but you I can impart:
Heaven, that is moved by you, my life has brought
   To where it stands, therefore I pray you heed
   What I shall say about the life I lead.

To you I tell the heart's new cares: always
   The sad Soul weeps within it, and there hears
   Voice of a Spirit that condemns her tears,
A Spirit that descends in your star's rays.
   Thought that once fed the grieving heart was sweet,
   Thought that oft fled up to your Father's feet.

There it beheld a Lady glorified,
   Of whom so sweetly it discoursed to me
   That the Soul said, "With her I long to be!"
Now One appears that drives the thought aside,
   And masters me with so effectual might
   That my heart quivers to the outward sight.

This on a Lady fixes my regard
   And says, "Who seeks where his salvation lies
   Must gaze intently in this Lady's eyes,
Nor dread the sighs of anguish!" O, ill-starred!
   Such opposite now breaks the humble dream
   Of the crowned angel in the glory beam.

Still, therefore, the Soul weeps, "The tender stir,"
   It says, "of thought that once consoled me flies!"
   That troubled one asks, "When into thine eyes
Looked she? Why doubted they my words of her?"
   I said, "Her eyes bear death to such as I:
   Yet, vainly warned, I gaze on her and die.

" Thou art not dead, but in a vain dismay,
   Dear Soul of ours so lost in thy distress,"
   Whispers a spirit voice of tenderness.
"This Lady's beauty darkens all your day,
   Vile fear possesses you; see, she is lowly,
   Pitiful, courteous, though so wise and holy.

" Think thou to call her Mistress evermore:
   Save thou delude thyself, then shall there shine
   High miracles before thee, so divine
That thou shalt say, O Love, when I adore,
   True Lord, behold the handmaid of the Lord,
   Be it unto me according to thy Word!"

My song, I do believe there will be few
   Who toil to understand thy reasoning;
   But if thou pass, perchance, to those who bring
No skill to give thee the attention due,
   Then pray I, dear last-born, let them rejoice
   To find at least a music in my voice.

CHAPTER I.

SINCE I, the servant, with preliminary discourse in the preceding Treatise, have with all due care prepared my bread, the time now summons, and requires my ship to leave the port: wherefore, having trimmed the mizen-mast of reason to the wind of my desire, I enter the ocean with the hope of an easy voyage, and a healthful happy haven to be reached at the end of my supper. But in order that my food may be more profitable, before the first dish comes on the table I wish to show how it ought to be eaten. I say then, as is narrated in the first chapter, that this exposition must be Literal and Allegorical; and to make this explicit one should know that it is possible to understand a book in four different ways, and that it ought to be explained chiefly in this manner.

The one is termed Literal, and this is that which does not extend beyond the text itself, such as is the fit narration of that thing whereof you are discoursing, an appropriate example of which is the third Song, which discourses of Nobility.

Another is termed Allegorical, and it is that which is concealed under the veil of fables, and is a Truth concealed under a beautiful Untruth; as when Ovid says that Orpheus with his lute made the wild beasts tame, and made the trees and the stones to follow him, which signifies that the wise man with the instrument of his voice makes cruel hearts gentle and humble, and makes those follow his will who have not the living force of knowledge and of art; who, having not the reasoning life of any knowledge whatever, are as the stones. And in order that this hidden thing should be discovered by the wise, it will be demonstrated in the last Treatise. Verily the theologians take this meaning otherwise than do the poets: but, because my intention here is to follow the way of the poets, I shall take the Allegorical sense according as it is used by the poets.

The third sense is termed Moral; and this is that which the readers ought intently to search for in books, for their own advantage and for that of their descendants; as one can espy in the Gospel, when Christ ascended the Mount for the Transfiguration, that, of the twelve Apostles, He took with Him only three. From which one can understand in the Moral sense that in the most secret things we ought to have but little company.

The fourth sense is termed Mystical, that is, above sense, supernatural; and this it is, when spiritually one expounds a writing which even in the Literal sense by the things signified bears express reference to the Divine things of Eternal Glory; as one can see in that Song of the Prophet which says that by the exodus of the people of Israel from Egypt Judæa is made holy and free. That this happens to be true according to the letter is evident. Not less true is that which it means spiritually, that in the Soul's liberation from Sin (or in the exodus of the Soul from Sin) it is made holy and free in its powers.

But in demonstrating these, the Literal must always go first, as that in whose sense the others are included, and without which it would be impossible and irrational to understand the others. Especially is it impossible in the Allegorical, because, in each thing which has a within and a without, it is impossible to come to the within if you do not first come to the without. Wherefore, since in books the Literal meaning is always external, it is impossible to reach the others, especially the Allegorical, without first coming to the Literal. Again, it is impossible, because in each thing, natural and artificial, it is impossible to proceed to the form without having first laid down the matter upon which the form should be. Thus, it is impossible for the form of the gold to come, if the matter, that is, its subject, is not first laid down and prepared; or for the form of the ark to come, if the material, that is, the wood, be not first laid down and prepared. Therefore, since the Literal meaning is always the subject and the matter of the others, especially of the Allegorical, it is impossible to come first to the meaning of the others before coming to it. Again, it is impossible, because in each thing, natural and artificial, it is impossible to proceed unless the foundation be first laid, as in the house, so also in the mind. Therefore, since demonstration must be the building up of Knowledge, and Literal demonstration must be the foundation of the other methods of interpreting, especially of the Allegorical, it is impossible to come first to the others before coming to that. Again, if it were possible that it could be so ordered, it would be irrational, that is, out of order ; and, therefore, one would proceed with much fatigue and with much error. Hence, as the Philosopher says in the first book of the Physics, Nature desires that we proceed in due order in our search for knowledge, that is, by proceeding from that which we know well to that which we know not so well; so I say that Nature desires it, inasmuch as this way to knowledge is innate in us ; and therefore, if the other meanings, apart from the Literal, are less understood—which they are, as evidently appears—it would be irrational to demonstrate them if the Literal had not first been demonstrated.

I, then, for these reasons will discourse in due order of each Song, firstly upon its Literal meaning, and after that I will discourse of its Allegory, that is, the hidden Truth, and sometimes I will touch incidentally on the other meanings as may be convenient to place and time.

CHAPTER II.

BEGINNING, then, I say that the star of Venus had twice revolved in that circle which causes the evening and the morning to appear, according to the two varying seasons, since the death of that blessed Beatrice, who lives in Heaven with the Angels, and on Earth with my soul; when that gentle Lady, of whom I made mention at the end of the "Vita Nuova," first appeared before my eyes, accompanied by Love, and assumed a position in my mind. And, as has been stated by me in the little book referred to, more because of her gentle goodness than from choice of mine, it befell that I consented to be her servant. For she appeared impassioned with such sorrow for my sad widowed life that the spirits of my eyes became especially friendly to her; and, so disposed, they then depicted her to be such that my good-will was content to espouse itself to that image. But because Love is not born suddenly, nor grows great nor comes to perfection in haste, but desires time and food for thought, especially there where there are antagonistic thoughts which impede it, there must needs be, before this new Love could be perfect, a great battle between the thought of its food and of that which was antagonistic to it, which still held the fortress of my mind for that glorious Beatrice. For the one was succoured on one side continually by the ever-present vision, and the other on the opposite side by the memory of the past. And the help of the ever-present sight increased each day, which memory could not do, in opposing that which to a certain degree prevented me from turning the face towards the past. Wherefore it seemed to me so wonderful, and also so hard to endure, that I could not support it, and with a loud cry (to excuse myself from the struggle, in which it seemed to me that I had failed in courage) I lifted up my voice towards that part whence came the victory of the new thought, which was full of virtuous power, even the power of celestial virtue; and I began to say: "You! who the third Heaven move, intent of thought." For the intelligent understanding of which Song, one must first know its divisions well, so that it will then be easy to perceive its meaning.

In order that it may no longer be necessary to preface the explanations of the others, I say that the order which will be taken in this Treatise I intend to keep through all the others. I say, then, that the proposed Song is contained within three principal parts. The first is the first verse of that, in which certain Intelligences are induced to listen to what I intend to say, or rather by a more usual form of speech we should call them Angels, who are in the revolution of the Heaven of Venus, as the movers thereof. The second is in the lines which follow after the first, in which is made manifest that which I felt spiritually amidst various thoughts. The third is in the last lines, wherein the man begins to speak to the work itself, as if to comfort it, as it were, and all these three parts are in due order to be demonstrated, as has been said above.

CHAPTER III.

THAT we may more easily perceive the Literal meaning of the first division, to which we now attend, it is requisite to know who and what are those who are summoned to my audience, and what is that third Heaven which I say is moved by them. And firstly I will speak of the Heaven; then I will speak of those whom I address. And although with regard to the truth concerning those things it is possible to know but little, yet so much as human reason can discern gives more delight than the best known and most certain of the things judged by the sense; according to the opinion of the Philosopher in his book on Animals.

I say, then, that concerning the number of the Heavens and their site, different opinions are held by many, although the truth at last may be found. Aristotle believed, following merely the ancient foolishness of the Astrologers, that there might be only eight Heavens, of which the last one, and which contained all, might be that where the fixed stars are, that is, the eighth sphere, and that beyond it there could be no other. Again, he believed that the Heaven of the Sun might be immediate with that of the Moon, that is, second to us. And this opinion of his, so erroneous, he who wishes can see in the second book on Heaven and the World, which is in the second of the Books on Natural History. In fact, he excuses himself for this in the twelfth book of the Metaphysics, where he clearly proves himself to have followed also another opinion where he was obliged to speak of Astrology. Ptolemy, then, perceiving that the eighth sphere is moved by many movements, seeing its circle to depart from the right circle, which turns from East to West, constrained by the principles of Philosophy, which of necessity desires a Primum Mobile, a most simple one, supposed another Heaven to be outside the Heaven of the fixed stars, which might make that revolution from East to West which I say is completed in twenty-four hours nearly, that is, in twenty-three hours, fourteen parts of the fifteen of another, counting roughly. Therefore, according to him, and according to that which is held in Astrology and in Philosophy since those movements were seen, there are nine moveable Heavens; the site of which is evident and determined, according to an Art which is termed Perspective, Arithmetical and Geometrical, by which and by other sensible experiences it is visibly and reasonably seen, as in the eclipses of the Sun it appears sensibly, that the Moon is below the Sun; and as by the testimony of Aristotle, who saw with his own eyes, according to what he says in the second book on Heaven and the World, the Moon, being new, to enter below Mars, on the side not shining, and Mars to remain concealed so long that he re-appeared on the other bright side of the Moon, which was towards the West.

CHAPTER IV.

AND the order of the houses is this, that the first that they enumerate is that where the Moon is; the second is that where Mercury is; the third is that where Venus is; the fourth is that where the Sun is; the fifth is that where Mars is; the sixth is that where Jupiter is; the seventh is that where Saturn is; the eighth is that of the Stars; the ninth is that which is not visible except by that movement which is mentioned above, which they designate the great Crystalline sphere, diaphanous, or rather all transparent. Truly, beyond all these, the Catholics place the Empyrean Heaven, which is as much as to say, the Heaven of Flame, or rather the Luminous Heaven; and they assign it to be immoveable, in order to have in itself, according to each part, that which its material desires. And this is why that first moved—the Primum Mobile—has such extremely rapid motion. For, because of the most fervent appetite which each part of it has to be united with each part of that most Divine Heaven of Peace, in which it revolves with so much desire, its velocity is almost incomprehensible. And this quiet and peaceful Heaven is the place of that Supreme Deity who from above beholds the whole. This is the place of the blessed Spirits, according as Holy Church teaches, which cannot speak falsely; and even Aristotle seems to feel this, to him who understands him well, in the first book of Heaven and the World. This is the highest bound of the World, within which the whole World is included, and beyond which there is nothing. And it is in no place, but was formed alone in the First Mind, which the Greeks term Protonoë. This is that magnificence of which the Psalmist spoke when he sang to God: "Thy glory is raised above the Heavens."

So, then, gathering together this which is discussed, it seems that there may be ten Heavens, of which the Heaven of Venus may be the third; whereof mention is made in that part which I intend to demonstrate. And it is to be known that each Heaven below the Crystalline has two firm poles as to itself; and the ninth has them firm and fixed, and not mutable in any respect. And each one, the ninth even as the others, has a circle, which one may term the equator of its own Heaven ; which equally, in each part of its revolution, is remote from one pole and from the other, as he who rolls an apple or any other round thing can sensibly perceive. And this circle has more swiftness in its movement than any other part of its Heaven, in each Heaven, as he may perceive who considers well. And each part, in proportion as it is nearer to it, moves so much the more swiftly; so much the slower in proportion as it is more remote and nearer to the pole; since its revolution is less, and it must of necessity be in one self-same time with the greater. I say again, that in proportion as the Heaven is nearer to the equatorial circle, so much the more noble is it in comparison to its poles; since it has more motion and more actuality and more life and more form and more touch from that which is above itself, and consequently has more virtue. Hence the stars in the Heaven of the fixed stars are more full of power amongst themselves in proportion as they are nearer to that circle.

And upon the back of this circle in the Heaven of Venus, of which I now speak, is a little sphere, which revolves by itself in this Heaven, the circle of which Astrologers call Epicycle ; and as the great sphere revolves about two poles, so does this little sphere: and so has this little sphere the equatorial circle ; and so much the more noble it is in proportion as it is nearer to those: and in the arc, or rather back, of this circle is fixed the most brilliant star of Venus. And, although it may be said that there are ten

Heavens according to strict Truth, this number does not comprehend them all: for that of which mention is made, the Epicycle, in which the star is fixed, is a Heaven by itself, or rather sphere; and it has not one essence with that which bears it, although it may be more like to it than to the others, and with it is called one Heaven, and they name the one and the other from the star. How the other Heavens and the other stars may be is not for present discussion; let it suffice that the nature of the third Heaven, with which I am at present concerned, has been told, and concerning which all that is at present needful has been shown.

CHAPTER V.

SINCE it has been shown in the preceding chapter what this third Heaven is, and how it is ordered in itself, it remains to show who those are who move it. It is then to be known, in the first place, that the movers thereof are substances apart from material, that is, Intelligences, which the common people term Angels: and of these creatures, as of the Heavens, different persons have had different ideas, although the truth may be found. There were certain Philosophers, of whom Aristotle appears to be one in his Metaphysics, although in the first book on Heaven and Earth incidentally he appears to think otherwise, who only believed these to be so many as there are revolutions in the Heavens, and no more; saying, that the others would have been eternally in vain, without operation, which was impossible, inasmuch as their being is their operation. There were others, like Plato, a most excellent man, who place not only so many Intelligences as there are movements in Heaven, but even as there are species of things, that is, manners of things; as of one species are all mankind, and of another all the gold, and of another all the silver, and so with all: and they are of opinion that as the Intelligences of the Heavens are generators of those movements each after his kind, so these were generators of the other things, each one being a type of its species: and Plato calls them *Ideas*, which is as much as to say, so many universal forms and natures.

The Gentiles called them Gods and Goddesses, although they could not understand those so philosophically as Plato did; and they adored their images, and built large temples to them, as to Juno, whom they called the Goddess of Power; as to Vulcan, whom they called the God of Fire; as to Pallas, or rather Minerva, whom they called the Goddess of Wisdom; and to Ceres, whom they called the Goddess of Corn. Opinions such as these the testimony of the Poets makes manifest, for they describe to a certain extent the mode of the Gentiles both in their sacrifices and in their faith; and it is testified also in many names, remains of antiquity, or in names of places and ancient buildings, as he who will can easily find. And although these opinions above mentioned might be built upon a good foundation by human reason and by no slight knowledge, yet the Truth was not seen by them, either from defect of reason or from defect of instruction. Yet even by reason it was possible to see that very numerous were the creatures above mentioned who are not such as men can understand. And the one reason is this: no one doubts, neither Philosopher, nor Gentile, nor Jew, nor Christian, nor any one of any sect, that they are either the whole or the greater part full of all Blessedness, and that those blessed ones are in a most perfect state. Therefore, since that which is here Human Nature may have not only one Beatitude, but two Beatitudes, as that of the Civil Life and that of the Contemplative, it would be irrational if we should see these Celestial Beings to have the Beatitude of the Active Life, that is, the Civil, in the government of the World, and not to have that of the Contemplative, which is the most excellent and most Divine.

But since that which has the Beatitude of the Civil government cannot have the other, because their intellect is one and perpetual, there must be others beyond this ministry, who live only in contemplation. And because this latter life is more Divine—and in proportion as the thing is more Divine so much the more is it in the image of God— it is evident that this life is more beloved of God: and if it be more beloved, so much the more vast has its Beatitude been; and if it has been more vast, so much the more vivifying power has He given to it rather than to the other; therefore one concludes that there may be a much larger number of those creatures than the effects tend to show. And this is not opposed to that which Aristotle seems to state in the tenth book of the Ethics, that to the separate substances the Contemplative Life must be requisite; as also the Active Life must be imperative to them. Nevertheless, in the contemplation of certain truths the revolution of the Heaven follows, which is the government of the World; which is, as it were, a Civil government ordained and comprehended in the contemplation of the movers, that is, the ruling Intelligences. The other reason is, that no effect is greater than the cause, because the cause cannot give that which it has not; wherefore, since the Divine Intellect is the cause of all, especially of the Human Intellect, it follows that the Human Intellect does not dominate the Divine, but is dominated by it in proportion to the superior power of the Divine. Hence, if we, by the reason above stated, and by many others, understand God to have been able to create Spiritual Creatures almost innumerable, it is quite evident that He has made them in this great number. Many other reasons it were possible to see: but let these suffice for the present. Nor let any one marvel if these and other reasons which we could adduce concerning this are not fully demonstrated; since likewise we ought to wonder at their excellence, which overpowers the eyes of the Human Mind, as the Philosopher says in the second book of the Metaphysics, and he affirms their existence. Though we have not any perception of them from which our knowledge can begin, yet some light from their most vivacious essence shines upon our intellect, inasmuch as we perceive the abovementioned reasons and many others, even as he who has the eyes closed affirms the air to be luminous, because of some little brightness or ray of light which passes through the pupils; as it is with the bat, for not otherwise are the eyes of the intellect closed, so long as the soul is bound and prisoned by the organs of our body.

CHAPTER VI.

It has been said that, through defective instruction, the ancients saw not the Truth concerning the Spiritual Creatures, although the people of Israel were in part instructed by their Prophets, through whom by many modes of speech and in many ways God had spoken to them, as the Apostle says. But we are therein instructed by Him who came from God, by Him who made them, by Him who preserves them, that is, by the Emperor of the Universe, who is Christ the Son of the Supreme God, and the Son of the Virgin Mary, a woman truly, and the daughter of Joseph and Anna—very Man, who was slain by us in order that He might bring us Life; who was the Light which enlightens us in the Darkness, even as John the Evangelist says; and He told us the Truth of those things which we could not have known without Him, nor seen truly. The first thing and the first secret which He showed us was one of the before-mentioned Beings or creatures. This was that one, His great Legate, the Angel Gabriel, who came to Mary, a young damsel of thirteen years, on the part of the Heavenly Saviour. This our Saviour, with His own mouth, said, that the Father could give Him many Legions of Angels. This He denied not, when it was said to Him that the Father had commanded His Angels that they should minister unto Him and should serve Him. Wherefore, it is evident to us that these creatures are in a very great number; since His Spouse and Secretary, Holy Church, of whom Solomon says: "Who is this that cometh forth from the Desert, full of those things which give delight, leaning upon her friend?" says, believes, and preaches these most noble creatures to be almost innumerable; and She divides them into three Hierarchies, that is to say, three holy, or rather Divine, Principalities: and each Hierarchy has three orders, so that nine orders of spiritual creatures the Church holds and affirms.

The first is that of the Angels, the second of the Archangels, the third of the Thrones; and these three orders make the first Hierarchy—not first as to nobility, nor as to creation, for the others are more noble, and all were created together, but first in degree, according to our perception of their exaltation.

Then there are the Dominations; after them the Virtues; then the Principalities; and these make the second Hierarchy.

Above these are the Powers and the Cherubim, and above all are the Seraphim; and these make the third Hierarchy.

And the most potent reason for their contemplation is the number in which the Hierarchies are, and that in which the orders are. For, since the Divine Majesty is in Three Persons, which have one substance, it is possible to contemplate them triply. For it is possible to contemplate the Supreme Power of the Father, which the first Hierarchy gazes upon, namely, that which is first by nobility, and which we enumerate last. And it is possible to contemplate the Supreme Wisdom of the Son; and upon this the second Hierarchy gazes. And it is possible to contemplate the Supreme and most fervent Charity of the Holy Spirit; and upon this the third Hierarchy gazes, which, being nearest to us, gives of the gifts which it receives.

And, since it is possible to regard each person in the Divine Trinity triply, so in each Hierarchy there are three orders which contemplate diversely. It is possible to consider the Father having regard to none but Him; and this is the contemplation of the Seraphim, who see more of the First Cause than any other Angelic Nature. It is possible to consider the Father according as He has relation to the Son, that is, how He is apart from Him, and how united with Him; and this is the contemplation of the Cherubim. It is possible again to consider the Father according as from Him proceeds the Holy Spirit, and how it is apart from Him and how united with Him; and this is the contemplation of the Powers.

And in like way it is possible to contemplate the Son and the Holy Spirit.

Wherefore, there must be nine orders of contemplative Spirits to gaze into the Light, which alone beholds itself completely. And this is not the place to be silent so much as one word. I say, that of all these orders some were lost as soon as they were created, perhaps in number of the tenth part, to restore which Human Nature was created. The numbers, the orders, the Hierarchies, declare the glory of the movable Heavens, which are nine; and the tenth announces this Unity and stability of God. And therefore the Psalmist says: "The Heavens declare the glory of God, and the Firmament showeth His handiwork." Wherefore it is reasonable to believe that the movers of the Heaven of the Moon are of the order of the Angels, and those of Mercury may be the Archangels, and those of Venus may be the Thrones, in whom the Love of the Holy Spirit being innate, they do their work conformably to it, which means that the revolution of that Heaven is full of Love. The form of the said Heaven takes from this a virtue by whose glow souls here below are kindled to love according to their disposition.

And because the ancients perceived that Heaven to be here below the cause of Love, they said that Love was the son of Venus, as Virgil testifies in the first book of the Æneid, where Venus says to Love: "Oh! son, my virtue, son of the great Father, who takest no heed of the darts of Typhœus." And Ovid so testifies in the fifth book of his Metamorphoses, when he says that Venus said to Love: "Son, my arms, my power." And there are Thrones which are ordered to the government of this Heaven in number not great, concerning which the Philosophers and the Astrologers have thought differently, according as they held different opinions concerning its revolutions. But all may be agreed, as many are, in this, as to how many movements it makes. Of this, as abbreviated in the book of the Aggregation of the Stars, you may find in the better demonstration of the Astrologers that there are three: one, according as the star moves towards its Epicycle; the other, according as the Epicycle moves with its whole Heaven equally with that of the Sun; the third, according as the whole of that Heaven moves, following the movement of the starry sphere from West to East in one hundred years one degree. So that to these Three Movements there are Three Movers. Again, if the whole of this Heaven moves and turns with the Epicycle from East to West once in each natural day, that movement, whether it be caused by some Intelligence or whether it be through the rapid movement of the Primum Mobile, God knows, for to me it seems presumptuous to judge.

These Movers produce, caring for that alone, the revolution proper to that sphere which each one moves. The most noble form of the Heaven, which has in itself the principle of this passive Nature, revolves, touched by the Moving Power, which cares for this; and I say touched, not by a bodily touch, but by a Power which directs itself to that operation. And these Movers are those to whom I begin to speak and to whom I put my inquiry.

CHAPTER VII.

ACCORDING to that which is said above in the third chapter of this treatise, in order to understand well the first part of the Song I comment on, it is requisite to discourse of those Heavens, and of their Movers; and in the three preceding chapters this has been discussed. I say, then, to those whom I proved to be Movers of the Heaven of Venus: "Ye who, with thought intent" (*i.e.*, with the intellect alone, as is said above), "the third Heaven move, Hear reasoning that is within my heart;" and I do not say "Hear" because they hear any sound, for they have no sense of hearing; but I say "Hear," meaning with that hearing which they have, which is of the understanding through the intellect. I say, "Hear reasoning that is within my heart," within me, which as yet has not appeared externally. It is to be known that throughout this Song, according to the one sense (the Literal), and the other sense (the Allegorical), the Heart is concerned with the secret within, and not any other special part of the soul or body. When I have called them to hear that which I wish to say, I assign two reasons why I ought fitly to speak to them. One is the novelty of my condition, which, from not having been experienced by other men, would not be so understood by them as by those who superintend such effects in their operation. And this reason I touch upon when I say: "To you alone its new thoughts I impart." The other reason is: when a man receives a benefit or injury, he ought first to relate it to him who bestows or inflicts it, if he can, rather than to others; in order that, if it be a benefit, he who receives it may show himself grateful towards the benefactor, and, if it be an injury, let him lead the doer thereof to gentle mercy with sweet words. And this reason I touch upon when I say: "Heaven, that is moved by you, my life has brought To where it stands;" that is to say, your operation, namely, your revolution, is that which has drawn me into the present condition; therefore I conclude and say that my speech ought to be to them, such as is said; and I say here: "Therefore to you 'tis need That I should speak about the life I lead." And after these reasons assigned, I beseech them to listen when I speak.

But, because in each manner of speech the speaker especially ought to look to persuasion, that is, to the pleasing of the audience, as that which is the beginning of all other persuasions, as do the Rhetoricians, and the most powerful persuasion to render the audience attentive is to promise to say new and wonderful things, I add to the prayer made for attention, this persuasion, or embellishment, announcing to them my intention to speak of new things, that is, the division which is in my mind; and great things, namely, the power of their star; and I say this in those last words of this first part:

> To you I'll tell the heart's new cares: always
>   The sad Soul weeps within it, and there hears
>   . Voice of a Spirit that condemns her tears,
> A Spirit that descends through your star's rays.

And to the full understanding of these words, I say that this Spirit is no other than a frequent thought how to commend and beautify this new Lady. And this Soul is no other than another thought, accompanied with acquiescence, which, repudiating that Spirit, commends and beautifies the memory of that glorious Beatrice. But, again, because the last sentiment of the mind, acquiescence, is held by that thought which memory assisted, I call it the Soul, and the other the Spirit; as we are accustomed to call the City those who hold it, and not those who fight it, although the one and the other may be citizens. I say also, that this Spirit comes on the rays of the star, because one desires to know that the rays of each Heaven are the way by which their virtue descends into things here below. And since the rays are no other than a light which comes from the source of Light through the air even to the thing illuminated, and the light has no source except the star, because the other Heaven is transparent, I say not that this Spirit, this thought, comes from their Heaven entirely, but from their star. And their star, through the nobility of its Movers, is of such virtue that in our souls, and in other things, it has very great power, notwithstanding that it is so far from us, about one hundred and sixty-seven times farther than it is to the centre of the Earth, which is three thousand two hundred and fifty miles.

And this is the Literal exposition of the first part of the Song.

CHAPTER VIII.

WHAT I have said shows clearly enough the Literal meaning of the first part. In the second, there is to be understood how it makes manifest what I experienced from the struggle within me; and this part has two divisions. In the first place it describes the quality of these oppositions, according as their cause was within me. Then I narrate what the one and the other voice of opposition said; and upon that firstly which described what was being lost, in the passage which is the second of that part and the third of the Song. In evidence, then, of the meaning of the first division, it is to be known that things must be named by that part of their form which is the noblest and best, as Man by Reason, and not by Sense, nor by aught else which is less noble; therefore, [when one speaks of the living man, one should understand the man using Reason, which is his especial Life, and is the action of his noblest part. And, therefore, whoso departs from Reason and uses only the Senses is not a living man, but a living beast, as says that most excellent Boëthius, "Let the Ass live."]

Rightly I speak, because thought is the right act of reason, wherefore the beasts who have it not do not think; and I speak not only of the lesser beasts, but of those who have a human appearance with the spirit of a sheep or of some other abominable beast. I say then: "Thought that once fed my grieving heart" —thought, that is, of the inner life—"was sweet"

(sweet, insomuch as it is persuasive, that is, pleasing, or beautiful, gentle, delightful); this thought often sped away to the feet of the Father of those Spirits to whom I speak, that is, God; that is to say, that I in thought contemplated the realm of the Blessed. "Thought that once fled up to the Father's feet." And I name the final cause immediately, because I ascended there above in thought when I say, "There I beheld a Lady glorified," to let you understand that I was certain, and am certain by its gracious revelation, that she was in Heaven; wherefore I, thinking many times how this was possible for me, went thither, rapt, as it were. Then subsequently I speak of the effect of this thought, in order to let you understand its sweetness, which was such that it made me desirous of Death, that I also might go where she was gone. And of this I speak there: "Of whom so sweetly it discoursed to me That the Soul said, 'With her would I might be!'" And this is the root of one of the struggles which was in me. And it is to be known that here one terms Thought, and not Soul, that which ascended to see that Blessed Spirit, because it was an especial thought sent on that mission; the Soul is understood, as is stated in the preceding chapter, as thought in general, with acquiescence.

Then, when I say, "Now One appears that drives the thought aside," I touch the root of the other struggle, saying how that previous thought was wont to be the life of me, even as another appears, which makes that one cease to be. I say, "drives the thought aside," in order to show that one to be antagonistic, for naturally the opposing one drives aside the other, and that which is driven appears to yield through want of power. And I say that this thought, which newly appears, is powerful in taking hold of me and in subduing my Soul, saying that it "masters me with such effectual might" that the heart, that is, my inner life, trembles so much that my countenance shows it in some new appearance.

Subsequently I show the power of this new thought by its effect, saying that it makes me "fix my regard" on a Lady, and speaks to me words of allurement, that is to say, it reasons before the eyes of my intelligent affection, in order the better to induce me, promising me that the sight of her eyes is its salvation. And in order to make this credible to the Soul experienced in love, it says that it is for no one to gaze into the eyes of this woman who fears the anguish of laboured sighs. And it is a beautiful mode of rhetoric when externally it appears that you disembellish a thing, and yet really embellish it within. This new thought of love could not induce my mind to consent, except by discoursing of the virtue of the eyes of this fair Lady so profoundly.

CHAPTER IX.

Now that it is shown how and whereof Love is born, and the antagonist that fought with me, I must proceed to open the meaning of that part in which different thoughts contend within me. I say that, firstly, one must speak on the part of the Soul, that is, of the former thought, and then of the other; for this reason, that always that which the speaker intends most especially to say he ought to reserve in the background, because that which is said finally, remains most in the mind of the hearer. Therefore, since I mean to speak further, and to discourse of that which performs the work of those to whom I speak, rather than of that which undoes this work, it was reasonable first to mention and to discourse of the condition of the part which was undone, and then of that which was generated by the other.

But here arises a doubt, which is not to be passed over without explanation. It would be possible for any one to say: Since Love is the effect of these Intelligences, to whom I speak, and that of the first Love might be the same as that of the new Love, why should their virtue destroy the one, and produce the other? since it ought to preserve the first, for the reason that each cause loves its effect, and ought to protect what it loves. To this question one can easily reply, that the effect of those Spirits, as has been said, is Love: and since they could not save it except in those who are subject to their revolution, they transfer it from that part which is beyond their power to that which is within reach, from the soul departed out of this life, into that which is yet living; as human nature transfers in the human form its preservation of the father to the son, because it cannot in this father preserve perpetually its effect: I say <u>effect</u> in as far as soul and body are united, and not effect in as far as that soul, which is divided from the body, lasts for ever, in a nature more than human. And thus is the question solved.

But since the immortality of the Soul is here touched upon, I will make a digression upon that; because to discourse of that will make a fit conclusion to the mention I have made of that living and blessed Beatrice, of whom I do not intend to speak further in this book.

For proposition I say that, amongst all the bestialities, that is the most foolish, the most vile, and most damnable which believes no other life to be after this life; wherefore, if we turn over all books, whether of philosophers or of the other wise writers, all agree in this, that in us there is some everlasting principle. And this especially Aristotle seems to desire in that book on the Soul; this especially each stoic seems to desire; this Tullius seems to desire, especially in that book on Old Age. This each of the Poets who have spoken according to the faith of the Gentiles seems to desire; this the law seems to desire, among Jews, Saracens, and Tartars, and all other people who live according to some civil law. And if all these could be deceived, there would result an impossibility which even to describe would be horrible. Each man is certain that human nature is the most perfect of all natures here below. This no one denies: and Aristotle affirms it when he says, in the twelfth book On Animals, that man is the most perfect of all the animals. Therefore, since many who live are entirely mortal, as are the brute animals, and all may be, whilst they live, without that hope of the other life; if our hope should be in vain, our want would be greater than that of any other animal. There have been many who have given this life for that: and thus it would follow that the most perfect animal, man, would be the most imperfect, which is impossible; and that that part, namely, reason, which is his chief perfection, would be in him the cause of the chief defect: which seems strange to say of the whole. And again it would follow that

Nature, in contradiction to herself, could have put this hope in the human mind ; since it is said that many have hastened to death of the body that they might live in the other life ; and this also is impossible. Again, we have continual experience of our immortality in the divination of our dreams, which could not be if there were no immortal part in us, since immortal must be the revelation. This part may be either corporeal or incorporeal if one think well and closely. I say corporeal or incorporeal, because of the different opinions which I find concerning this. That which is moved, or rather informed, by an immediate informer, ought to have proportion to the informer ; and between the mortal and the immortal there is no proportion. Again, we are assured of it by the most truthful doctrine of Christ, which is the Way, the Truth, and the Light : the Way, because by it without impediment we go to the happiness of that immortality ; the Truth, because it endures no error ; the Light, because it enlightens us in the darkness of worldly ignorance. This doctrine, I say, which above all other reasons makes us certain of it ; for it has been given to us by Him who sees and measures our immortality, which we cannot perfectly see whilst our immortal is mingled with the mortal. But we see it by faith perfectly ; and by reason we see it with the cloud of obscurity which grows from the mixture of the mortal with the immortal. This ought to be the most powerful argument that both are in us : and I thus believe, thus affirm ; and I am equally certain, after this life, to pass to that other and better life—there where that glorious Lady lives, with whom my soul was enamoured when it was struggling, as will be set forth in the next chapter.

CHAPTER X.

Returning to the proposition, I say that in that verse which begins "A foe so strong I find him that he destroys," I intend to make manifest that which was discoursing in my Soul, the ancient thought against the new; and first briefly I show the cause of its lamentation, when I say: "This opposite now breaks the humble dream Of the crowned angel in the glory-beam." This one is that especial thought of which it is said above that it was wont to be the life of the sorrowing heart. Then when I say, "Still, therefore, my Soul weeps," it is evident that my Soul is still on its side, and speaks with sadness; and I say that it speaks words of lamentation, as if it might wonder at the sudden transformation, saying: "'The tender star,' It says, 'that once was my consoler, flies.'" It can well say consoler, for in the great loss which I sustained in the death of Beatrice this thought, which ascended into Heaven, had given to my Soul much consolation.

Then afterwards I say, that all my thought, my Soul, of which I say, "That troubled one," turns in excuse of itself, and speaks against the eyes; and this is made evident there: "That troubled one asked, 'When into thine eyes Looked she?'" And I say that she speaks of them and against them three things: the first is, she blasphemes the hour when this woman saw them. And here you must know, that although many things in one hour can come into the eyes, truly that which comes by a straight line into the point of the pupil, that truly one sees, and that only is sealed in the imaginative part. And this is, because the nerve by which the visible spirit runs is directed to that part, and thereupon truly one eye cannot look on the eye of another so that it is not seen by it; for as that which looks receives the form of the pupil by a right line, so by that same line its form passes into that eye which gazes. And many times in the direction of that line a shaft flies from the bow of Love, with whom each weapon is light. Therefore, when I ask, "When first into mine eyes looked she?" it is as much as to ask, "When did her eyes and mine look into each other?"

The second point is in that which reproves their disobedience, when it says, "Of her, why doubted they my words?" Then it proceeds to the third thing and says that it is not right to reprove them for precaution, but for their disobedience; for it says that, sometimes, when speaking of this woman, it might be said, "Her eyes bear death to such as I," if she could have opened the way of approach. And indeed one ought to believe that my Soul knew of its own inclination ready to receive the operation of this power, and therefore dreaded it; for the act of the agent takes full effect in the patient who has the inclination to receive it, as the Philosopher says in the second book on the Soul. And, therefore, if wax could have the spirit of fear, it would fear most to come into the rays of the Sun, which would not turn it into stone, since its disposition is to yield to that strong operation.

Lastly, the Soul reveals in its speech that their presumption had been dangerous when it says, "Yet vainly warned, I gazed on her and die." And thus it closes its speech, to which the new thought replies, as will be declared in the following chapter.

CHAPTER XI.

The meaning of that part in which the Soul speaks, that is, the old thought which is undone, has been shown. Now, in due order, the meaning must be shown of the part in which the new antagonistic thought speaks; and this part is contained entirely in the verse or stanza which begins, "Thou art not dead," which part, in order to understand it well, I will divide into two; that in the first part, which begins "Thou art not dead," it then says, continuing its last words, "It is not true that thou art dead; but the cause wherefore thou to thyself seemest to be dead is a deadly dismay into which thou art vilely fallen because of this woman who has appeared to thee." And here it is to be observed that, as Boëthius says in his Consolation, each sudden change of things does not happen without some flurry of mind. And this is expressed in the reproof of that thought which is called "the spirit voice of tenderness," when it gave me to understand that my consent was inclining towards it; and thus, one can easily comprehend this, and recognize its victory, when it already says, "Dear Soul of ours," therein making itself familiar. Then, as is stated, it commands where it ought to rebuke that Soul, in order to induce it to come to her; and therefore it says to her: "See, she is lowly, Pitiful, courteous, though so wise and holy."

These are two things which are a fit remedy for the fear with which the Soul appeared impassioned; for, firmly united, they cause the individual to hope well, and especially Pity, which causes all other goodness to shine forth by its light. Wherefore Virgil, speaking of Æneas, in his greater praise calls him compassionate, pitiful; and that is not pity such as the common people understand it, which is to lament over the misfortunes of others; nay, this is an especial effect which is called Mercy, Pity, Compassion; and it is a passion. But compassion is not a passion; rather a noble disposition of mind, prepared to receive Love, Mercy, and other charitable passions. Then it says: "See also how courteous, though so wise and holy."

Here it says three things which, according as they can be acquired by us, make the person especially pleasing. It says Wise. Now, what is more beautiful in a woman than knowledge? It says Courteous. Nothing in a woman can be more excellent than courtesy. And neither are the wretched common people deceived even in this word, for they believe that courtesy is no other than liberality; for liberality is an especial, and not a general courtesy. Courtesy is all one with honesty, modesty, decency; and because the virtues and good manners were the custom in Courts anciently, as now the opposite is the custom, this word was taken from the Courts; which word, if it should now be taken from the Courts, especially of Italy, would and could express no other than baseness. It says Holy. The greatness which is here meant is especially well accompanied with the two afore-mentioned virtues; because it is that light which reveals the good and the evil of the person clearly. And how much knowledge and how much virtuous custom does there not seem to be wanting by this light! How much madness and how much vice are seen to be by this light! Better would it be for the wretched madmen high in station, stupid and vicious, to be of low estate, that neither in the world nor after this life they should be so infamous. Truly for such Solomon says in Ecclesiastes: "There is a sore evil that I have seen under the Sun; namely, riches kept for the owners thereof to their hurt."

Then subsequently it lays a command on it, that is, on my Soul, that it should now call this one its Lady: "Think thou to call her Mistress evermore," promising my Soul that it will be quite content with her when it shall have clear perception of all her wonderful accomplishments; and then this one says: "Save thou delude thyself, then shall there shine High miracles before thee;" neither does it speak otherwise even to the end of that stanza. And here ends the Literal meaning of all that which I say in this Song, speaking to these Celestial Intelligences.

CHAPTER XII.

FINALLY, according to that which the letter of this Commentary said above, when I divided the principal parts of this Song, I turn back with the face of my discourse to the same Song, and I speak to that. And in order that this part may be understood more fully, I say that generally in each Song there is what is called a Tornata, because the Reciters, who originally were accustomed to compose it, so contrived that when the song was sung, with a certain part of the song they could return to it. But I have rarely done it with that intention; and, in order that others may perceive, this I have seldom placed it with the sequence of the Song, so long as it is in the rhythm which is necessary to the measure. But I have used it when it was requisite to express something independent of the meaning of the Song, and which was needful for its embellishment, as it will be possible to perceive in this and in the other Songs.

And, therefore, I say at present, that the goodness and the beauty of each discourse are parted and divided; for the goodness is in the meaning, and the beauty in the ornament of the words. And the one and the other are with delight, although the goodness is especially delightful. Wherefore, since the goodness of this Song might be difficult to perceive, because of the various persons who are led to speak in it, where so many distinctions are required; and the beauty would be easy to see, it seemed to me, of the nature of the Song that by some men more attention might be paid to the beauty of the words than to the goodness of matter. And this is what I say in that part.

But, because it often happens that to admonish seems presumptuous in certain conditions, it is usual for the Rhetorician to speak indirectly to others, directing his words, not to him for whom he speaks, but towards another. And truly this method is maintained here; for to the Song the words go, and to the men the meaning of them. I say then: "My Song, I do believe there will be few Who toil to understand thy reasoning." And I state the cause, which is double. First, because thou speakest with fatigue—with fatigue, I say, for the reason which is stated; and then because thou speakest with difficulty—with difficulty, I say, as to the novelty of the meaning. Now afterwards I admonish it, and say:

> But if thou pass perchance by those who bring
> No skill to give thee the attention due,
>   Then pray I, dear last-born, let them rejoice
>   At least to find a music in my voice.

For in this I desire to say no other according to what is said above, except "Oh, men, you who cannot see the meaning of this Song, do not therefore refuse it; but pay attention to its beauty, which is great, both for construction, which belongs to the Grammarians; and for the order of the discourse, which belongs to the Rhetoricians; as well as for the rhythm of its parts, which belongs to the Musicians." For which things he who looks well can see that there may be beauty in it. And this is the entire Literal meaning of the first Song which is prepared for the first dish in my Banquet.

CHAPTER XIII.

SINCE the Literal meaning has been sufficiently explained, we must now proceed to the Allegorical and true exposition. And, therefore, beginning again from the first head, I say that when I had lost the chief delight of my Soul in former time, I was left so stung with sadness that no consolation whatever availed me. Nevertheless, after some time, my mind, reasoning with itself to heal itself, took heed, since neither my own nor that of another availed to comfort it, to turn to the method which a certain disconsolate one had adopted when he looked for Consolation. And I set myself to read that book of Boëthius, not known to many, in which, when a captive exile, he had consoled himself. And, again, hearing that Tullius had written another book, in which, treating of Friendship, he had spoken words for the consolation of Lælius, a most excellent man, on the death of his friend Scipio, I set myself to read it. And although at first it was difficult to me to enter into their meaning, yet, finally, I entered into it so much as the knowledge of grammar that I possessed, together with some slight power of intellect, enabled me to do: by which power of intellect I formerly beheld many things almost like a person in a dream, as may be seen in the Vita Nuova. And as it is wont to be that a man goes seeking for silver, and beyond his purpose he finds gold, whose hidden cause appears not perhaps without the Divine Will; I, who sought to console myself, found not only a remedy for my tears, but words of authors and of sciences and of books; reflecting on which I judged well that Philosophy, who was the Lady of these authors, of these sciences, and of these books, might be a supreme thing. And I imagined her in the form of a gentle Lady; and I could imagine her in no other attitude than a compassionate one, because if willingly the sense of Truth beheld her, hardly could it turn away from her. And with this imagination I began to go where she is demonstrated truthfully, that is, to the Schools of the Religious, and to the disputations of the Philosophers; so that in a short time, perhaps of thirty months, I began to feel her sweetness so much that my love for her chased away and destroyed all other thought. Wherefore I, feeling myself to rise from the thought of the first Love to the virtue of this new one, as if wondering at myself, opened my mouth in the speech of the proposed Song, showing my condition under the figure of other things: for of the Lady with whom I was enamoured, no rhyme of any Vernacular was worthy to speak openly, neither were the hearers so well prepared that they could have easily understood the words without figure: neither would faith have been given by them to the true meaning, as to the figurative; since if the truth of the whole was believed, that I was inclined to that love, it would not be believed of this. I then begin to speak: "Ye who, intent of thought, the third Heaven move."

And because, as has been said, this Lady was the daughter of God, the Queen of all, the most noble and most beautiful Philosophy, it remains to be seen who these Movers were, and what this third Heaven. And firstly of the third Heaven, according to the order which has been gone through. And here it is not needful to proceed to division, and to explanation of the letter, for, having turned the fictitious speech away from that which it utters to that which it means, by the exposition just gone through, this meaning is sufficiently made evident.

CHAPTER XIV.

IN order to see what is meant by the "third Heaven," one has in the first place to perceive what I desire to express by this word Heaven alone: and then one will see how and why this third Heaven was needful to us. I say that by Heaven I mean Science, and by the Heavens "the Sciences," from three resemblances which the Heavens have with the Sciences, especially by the order and number in which they must appear; as will be seen by discussing that word Third. The first similitude is the revolution of the one and the other round one fixed centre. For each movable Heaven revolves round its centre, which, on account of its movement, moves not; and thus each Science moves round its subject, which itself moves not; for no Science demonstrates its own foundation, but presupposes that. The second similitude is the illumination of the one and the other. For each Heaven illuminates visible things; and thus each Science illuminates the things intelligible. And the third similitude is the inducing of perfection in the things so inclined. Of which induction, as to the first perfection, that is, of the substantial generation, all the philosophers agree that the Heavens are the cause, although they attribute this in different ways: some from the Movers, as Plato, Avicenna, and Algazel; some from the stars themselves, especially the human souls, as Socrates, and also Plato and Dionysius the Academician; and some from celestial virtue which is in the natural heat of the seed, as Aristotle and the other Peripatetics. Thus the Sciences are the cause in us of the induction of the second perfection; by the use of which we can speculate concerning the Truth, which is our ultimate perfection, as the Philosopher says in the sixth book of the Ethics, when he says that Truth is the good of the intellect. Because of these and many other resemblances, it is possible to call Science, Heaven.

Now it remains to see why it is called the third Heaven. Here it is requisite to reflect somewhat with regard to a comparison which exists between the order of the Heavens and that of the Sciences. Wherefore, as has been previously described, the Seven Heavens next to us are those of the Planets; then there are two Heavens above these, the Mobile; and one above all, Quiet. To the Seven first correspond the Seven Sciences of the *Trivium* and of the *Quadrivium*, namely, Grammar, Logic, Rhetoric,

Arithmetic, Music, Geometry, and Astrology. To the eighth Sphere, *i.e.*, to the starry, correspond Natural Science, which is termed Physics, and the first Science, which is termed Metaphysics. To the ninth Sphere corresponds Moral Science; and to the Quiet Heaven corresponds Divine Science, which is designated Theology.

And the reason why this is, remains briefly to be seen. I say that the Heaven of the Moon is likened unto Grammar because it is possible to find a comparison to it. For if you look at the Moon well, two things are seen to be proper to it which are not seen in the other stars: the one is the shadow which is in it, which is no other than the rarity of its body, in which the rays of the Sun can find no end wherefrom to strike back again as in the other parts; the other is the variation of its brightness, which now shines on one side, and now on the other, according as the Sun sees it. And these two properties Grammar has: for, because of its infinity, the rays of reason can find no end in it in parts, especially of the words; and it shines now on this side, now on that, inasmuch as certain words, certain declensions, certain constructions, are in use which were not formerly, and many formerly were which again will be; as Horace says in the beginning of his book on the art of Poetry, when he says: "Many words will spring up again which have now fallen out of use."

And the Heaven of Mercury may be compared to Logic because of two properties: that Mercury is the smallest star in Heaven, that the amount of its diameter is no more than two hundred and thirty-two miles, according as Alfergano puts it, who says that it is one twenty-eighth part of the diameter of the

Earth, which is six thousand five hundred miles; the other property is, that it is more concealed by the rays of the Sun than any other star. And these two properties are in Logic: for Logic is less in substance than any other Science, for it is perfectly compiled and terminated in so much text as is found in the old Art and the new; and it is more concealed than any other Science, inasmuch as it proceeds with more sophistical and probable arguments than any other.

And the Heaven of Venus may be compared to Rhetoric because of two properties: the one is the brightness of its aspect, which is most sweet to behold, far more than any other star; the other is its appearance, now in the morning, now in the evening. And these two properties are in Rhetoric: for Rhetoric is the sweetest of all Sciences, since it principally aims at sweetness. It appears in the morning, when the Rhetorician speaks before the face of the hearer; it appears in the evening, that is, afterwards, when it speaks by Letters in distant parts.

And the Heaven of the Sun may be compared to Arithmetic because of two properties: the one is, that with his light all the other stars are informed; the other is that the eye cannot gaze at it. And these two properties are in Arithmetic, which with its light illuminates all its Sciences: for their subjects are all considered under some Number, and with Number one always proceeds in the consideration of these; as in Natural Science the movable body is the subject, which movable body has in itself three reasons of continuity, and this has in itself reason of infinite number. And of Natural Science its first and chiefest consideration is to consider the principles of natural objects, which are three, that is, matter, privation, and form; in which this Number is seen, and not only in all together, but again in each one, as he who considers subtly may perceive. Wherefore, Pythagoras, according to what Aristotle says in the first book of the Physics, established as the principles of natural things, the equal and the unequal; considering all things to be Number. The other property of the Sun is again seen in Number, of which Number is the Science of Arithmetic, that the eye of the intellect cannot gaze at it. For Number, inasmuch as it is considered in itself, is infinite; and this we cannot understand.

And the Heaven of Mars may be compared to Music because of two properties. One is its most beautiful relative position; for, when enumerating the movable Heavens, from which one soever you may begin, either from the lowest or from the highest, this Heaven of Mars is the fifth; it is the central one of all, that is, of the first, of the second, of the third, and of the fourth. The other is, that this Mars dries up and burns things, because his heat is like to that of fire; and this is why it appears flaming in colour, sometimes more and sometimes less, according to the density and rarity of the vapours which follow it, which of themselves are often kindled, as is determined in the first book on Meteors. And, therefore, Albumassar says that the kindling of these vapours signifies the death of Kings and the change of Kingdoms; for they are the effects of the dominion of Mars. And, therefore, Seneca says that, on the death of Augustus, he beheld on high a ball of fire. And in Florence, at the beginning of its destruction, there was seen in the air, in the form of a cross, a great quantity of these vapours following the planet

Mars. And these two properties are in Music, which is all relative, as is seen in harmonized words and in songs, from which the sweeter harmony results in proportion as the relation is more beautiful, which in this Science is especially beautiful, because there is in it a special harmony. Again, Music attracts to itself human spirits, which are as it were chiefly vapours from the heart, so that they almost cease from all labour; so is the whole soul when it hears it, and the power of all those spirits flies as it were to the spirit of sense, which receives the sound.

And the Heaven of Jupiter can be compared to Geometry because of two properties. The one is, that it moves between two Heavens, repugnant to its good tempering, namely, that of Mars and that of Saturn. Hence Ptolemy says, in the book alluded to, that Jupiter is a star of a temperate complexion, midway between the cold of Saturn and the heat of Mars. The other is, that amongst all the stars it appears white, as if silvered. And these things are in the Science of Geometry. Geometry moves between two things antagonistic to it; as between the point and the circle, and I term circle freely anything that is round, either a body or superfices; for, as Euclid says, the point is the beginning of Geometry, and, according to what he says, the circle is the most perfect figure in it, which must therefore have reason for its end; so that between the point and the circle, as between the beginning and the end, Geometry moves. And these two are antagonistic to its certainty; for the point by its indivisibility is immeasurable, and the circle, on account of its arc, it is impossible to square perfectly, and therefore it is impossible to measure precisely. And again, Geometry is most white, inasmuch as it is without spot of error, and it is most certain in itself, and by its handmaid, called Perspective.

And the Heaven of Saturn has two properties because of which it can be compared to Astrology. One is the slowness of its movement through the twelve signs; for twenty-nine years and more, according to the writings of the Astrologers, is the time that it requires in its orbit. The other is, that above all the other planets it is highest. And these two properties are in Astrology, for in completing its circle, as in the acquirement of this Science, the greatest space of time is revolved, because its demonstrations are more than any other of the aforementioned Sciences, and long experience is requisite to those who would acquire good judgment in it. And again, it is the highest of all the others, because, as Aristotle says in the commencement of his book on the Soul, the Science is high, because of its nobility, and because of the nobleness of its subject and its certainty. And this Science more than any other of those mentioned above is noble and high, for noble and high is its subject, which is the movement of the Heavens; and high and noble, because of its certainty, which is without any defect, even as that which springs from the most perfect and most regular principle. And if any one believe that there is defect in it, it is not on the part of the Science, but, as Ptolemy says, it is through our negligence, and to that it must be imputed.

CHAPTER XV.

AFTER the comparisons which I have made of the seven first Heavens, we must now proceed to the others, which are three, as has been often stated.

I say that the Starry Heaven may be compared to Physics because of three properties, and to Metaphysics because of three others. For it shows us of itself two visible things, such as the multitude of stars and such as the Galaxy, that white circle which the common people call the Path of St. James. It shows to us also one of the poles, and keeps the other hidden from us. And it shows to us one movement alone from East to West; and another, which it makes from West to East, it keeps almost, as it were, hidden from us. Therefore, in due order are to be seen, first the comparison with the Physical and then that with the Metaphysical.

I say that the Starry Heaven shows us many stars; for, according to what the wise men of Egypt have seen, even to the last star which appeared to them in the Meridian, they place there twenty-two thousand bodies of stars, of which I speak. And in this it has the greatest similitude with Physics, if these three numbers, namely, Two, and Twenty, and Thousand, are regarded well and subtly. For by the two is meant the local movement, which is of necessity from one point to another; and by the twenty is signified the movement of the alteration, for, since from the ten upwards one advances not except by altering this ten with the other nine and with itself; and the most beautiful alteration which it receives is its own with itself, and the first which it receives is the twenty; reasonably by this number the said movement is signified. And by the thousand is signified the movement of increase, which in name, that is, this thousand, is the greater number, and to increase still more is not possible except by multiplying this. And these three movements alone are observed in Physics, as it is demonstrated in the fifth chapter of his first book.

And because of the Milky Way, this Heaven has a great similitude with Metaphysics. Wherefore, it is to be known that concerning this Galaxy the Philosophers have had different opinions. For the followers of Pythagoras said that the Sun at some time or other went astray from his path, and, passing through other parts not suitable to his fervent heat, he burnt the place through which he passed, and there remained that appearance of the conflagration. And I believe that they were moved by the fable of Phaëton, which Ovid relates in the beginning of the second part of his Metamorphoses. Others said, such as Anaxagoras and Democritus, that it was the light of the Sun reflected into that part. And these opinions, with demonstrative reasons, they proved over and over again. What Aristotle may have said of this is not so easy to learn, because his opinion is not found to be the same in one translation as in the other; and I believe that it might be due to the error of the translators, for in the new one he seems to say that the Galaxy is a collection of vapours under the stars of that part which always attract them; and this does not seem to be the true reason. In the old translation he says that the Galaxy is no other than a multitude of fixed stars in that part, so small that we cannot distinguish them from here below, but that they cause the whiteness which we call the Milky Way. And it may be that the Heaven in that part is more dense, and therefore retains and represents that light; and this opinion Avicenna and Ptolemy seem to share with Aristotle. Therefore, since the Galaxy is an effect of those stars which we cannot see, if we understand those things by their effect alone, and Metaphysics treats of the first substances, which we cannot similarly understand except by their effects, it is evident that the Starry Heaven has a great similitude to Metaphysics.

Again, by the pole which we see is signified the things known to our senses, concerning which, taking them universally, the Science of Physics treats; and by the pole which we do not see is signified the things which are without matter, which are not sensible, concerning which Metaphysics treats; and therefore the said Heaven has a great similitude with the one Science and with the other.

Again, by the two movements it signifies these two Sciences: for by the movement in which every day revolves, and makes a new revolution from point to point, it signifies things natural and corruptible which daily complete their path, and their material is changed from form to form; and of this the Science of Physics treats. And by the almost insensible movement which it makes from West to East by one degree in a hundred years, it signifies things incorruptible, which received from God the beginning of their creation, and will have no end; but of these Metaphysics treats. Therefore I say that this movement signifies those things, for it began this revolution which will have no end; the end of the revolution being to return to one self-same point, to which this Heaven will not return by this movement, which has revolved a little more than the sixth part from the commencement of the world; and we are now in the last age of the world, and verily we wait the consummation of the celestial movement. Thus it is evident that the Starry Heaven, on account of many properties, may be compared to the Science of Physics and Metaphysics.

The Crystalline Heaven, which, as the Primum Mobile, has been previously counted, has a sufficiently evident comparison to Moral Philosophy; for Moral Philosophy, according to what Tommaso says upon the second book of the Ethics, teaches us method in the other Sciences.

For as the Philosopher says in the fifth book of the Ethics, legal Justice requires the Sciences to be learnt, and commands, in order that they may not be abandoned, that they be learnt and taught: thus, the said Heaven rules with its movement the daily revolution of all the others; from which revolution every day all those receive and send below the virtues of their several parts. For, if the revolution of this Heaven could not rule over that, but little of their power would descend below, and little of their aspect. Wherefore we hold that, if it could be possible for this ninth Heaven not to move, the third part of the Heaven would not again be seen in any part from the Earth: Saturn would be for fourteen years and a half concealed from any place on the Earth, Jupiter would be hidden for six years, and Mars for almost a whole year, and the Sun for one hundred and eighty-two days and fourteen hours (I say days, meaning so much time as so many days measure); and Venus and Mercury, almost like the Sun, would be hidden and would reappear, and the Moon for the space of fourteen days and a half would be hidden from all people. Verily, here below there would be neither generation, nor the life of animals, nor of plants; there would be no night, nor day, nor week, nor month, nor year; but the whole Universe would be disordered, and the movement of the stars would be in vain. Not otherwise, should Moral Philosophy cease to be, would the other Sciences be hidden for some time, and there would be no generation nor life of happiness, and all books would be in vain, and all discoveries of old. Therefore it is sufficiently evident that there is a comparison between this Heaven and Moral Philosophy.

Again, the Empyrean Heaven, because of its Peace, bears a similitude to the Divine Science, which is full of all Peace; which endures no conflict of opinion or of sophistical arguments, on account of the most excellent certainty of its subject, which is God. And of this He Himself speaks to His disciples: "My peace I give to you: My peace I leave unto you," giving and leaving to them His doctrine, which is this Science whereof I speak.

Solomon says of this Science: "Sixty are the queens, and eighty the friendly concubines; and youthful virgins without number; but one is my dove and my perfect one." All the Sciences he terms queens, and friends, and virgins; and he calls this one dove, because it is without blemish of strife; and he calls this one perfect, because it causes us to see perfectly the Truth in which our Soul finds Peace.

And therefore the comparison of the Heavens to the Sciences having been thus reasoned out, it is easy to see that by the Third Heaven I mean Rhetoric, which has been likened unto the Third Heaven, as appears above.

CHAPTER XVI.

By the similitudes spoken of it is possible to see who these Movers are to whom I speak; what are the Movers of that Heaven; even as Boëthius and Tullius, who by the sweetness of their speech sent me, as has before been stated, to the Love, which is the study of that most gentle Lady, Philosophy, by the rays of their star, which is the written word of that fair one. Therefore in each Science the written word is a star full of light, which that Science reveals. And, this being made manifest, it is easy to see the true meaning of the first verse of the purposed Poem by means of the exposition, Figurative and Literal. And by means of this self-same exposition one can sufficiently understand the second verse, even to that part where it says, This Spirit made me look on a fair Lady: where it should be known that this Lady is Philosophy; which truly is a Lady full of sweetness, adorned with modesty, wonderful for wisdom, the glory of freedom, as in the Third Treatise, where her Nobility will be described, it is made manifest. And then where it says: "Who seeks where his Salvation lies, Must gaze intently in this Lady's eyes;" the eyes of this Lady are her demonstrations, which look straight into the eyes of the intellect, enamour the Soul, and set it free from the trammels of circumstance. Oh, most sweet and ineffable forms, swift stealers of the human mind, which appear in these demonstrations, that is, in the eyes of Philosophy, when she discourses to her faithful friends! Verily in you is Salvation, whereby he is made blessed who looks at you, and is saved from the death of Ignorance and Vice. Where it says, "Nor dread the sighs of anguish, joys debarred," the wish is to signify, if he fear not the labour of study and the strife of conflicting opinions, which flow forth ever multiplying from the living Spring in the eyes of this Lady, and then her light still continuing, they fall away, almost like little morning clouds before the Sun. And now <u>the intellect, become her friend, remains free and full of certain Truth, even as the atmosphere is rendered pure and bright by the shining of the midday Sun.</u>

The third passage again is explained by the Literal exposition as far as to where it says, "Still therefore the Soul weeps." Here it is desirable to attend to a certain moral sense which may be observed in these words: that a man ought not for the sake of the greater friend to forget the service received from the lesser; but if one must follow the one and leave the ‚other, the greater is to be followed, with honest lamentation for desertion of the other, whereby he gives occasion to the one whom he follows to bestow more love on him. Then there where it says, "Of my eyes," has no other meaning except that bitter was the hour when the first demonstration of this Lady entered into the eyes of my <u>intellect</u>, which was the cause of this most close attachment. And there where it says, "My peers," it means the Souls set free from miserable and vile pleasures, and from vulgar habits, endowed with understanding and memory. And then it says, "Her eyes bear death," and then it says, "I gazed on her and die," which appears contrary to that which is said above of Salvation by this Lady. And therefore it is to be known that one Spirit speaks here on one side and the other speaks there on the other; which two dispute contrariwise, according to that which is made evident above. Wherefore it is no wonder if here the one Spirit says Yes, and there the other Spirit says No. Then in the stanza where it says, "A sweet voice of tenderness," a thought is meant which was born of my deep contemplation; wherefore it is to be known that by Love, in this Allegory, is always meant that deep contemplation which is the earnest application of the enamoured mind to that object wherewith it is enamoured. Then when it says, "There shall shine High miracles before thee," it announces that through her the adornments of the miracles will be seen; and it speaks truly, that the adornment of the miracles is to see the cause of the same, which she demonstrates; as in the beginning of the book on Metaphysics the Philosopher seems to feel, saying that, through the contemplation of these adornments, men began to be enamoured with this Lady. And concerning this word, *i.e.*, miracle, in the following treatise I shall speak more fully. What then follows of this Song is sufficiently explained by the other exposition.

And thus at the end of this Second Treatise, I say and affirm that the Lady with whom I became enamoured after the first Love was the most beautiful and most excellent daughter of the Ruler of the Universe, to which daughter Pythagoras gave the name of Philosophy. And here ends the Second Treatise, which is brought in for the first dish at my Banquet.

The Third Treatise.

LOVE, reasoning of my Lady in my mind
   With constant pleasure, oft of her will say
   Things over which the intellect may stray;
His words make music of so sweet a kind
   That the Soul hears and feels, and cries, Ah, me,
   That I want power to tell what thus I see!

If I would tell of her what thus I hear,
   First, all that Reason cannot make its own
   I needs must leave; and of what may be known
Leave part, for want of words to make it clear.
   If my Song fail, blame wit and words, whose force
   Fails to tell all I hear in Love's discourse.

The Sun sees not in travel round the earth,
   Till it reach her abode, so fair a thing
   As she of whom Love causes me to sing.
All minds of Heaven wonder at her worth;
   Mortals, enamoured, find her in their thought
   When Love his peace into their minds has brought.

Her Maker saw that she was good, and poured,
   Beyond our Nature, fulness of His Power
   On her pure soul, whence shone this holy dower
Through all her frame, with beauty so adored
   That from the eyes she touches heralds fly
   Heartward with longings, heavenward with a sigh.

On her fair frame Virtue Divine descends
   As on the angel that beholds His face.
   Fair one who doubt, go with her, mark the grace
In all her acts. Downward from Heaven bends
   An angel when she speaks, who can attest
   A power in her by none of us possessed.

The graceful acts that she shows forth to all
   Rival in calls to love that love must hear;
   Fair in all like her, fairest she'll appear
Who is most like her. We, content to call
   Her face a Miracle, have Faith made sure:
   For that, He made her ever to endure.

Her aspect shows delights of Paradise,
   Seen in her eyes and in her smiling face;
   Love brought them there as to his dwelling-place.
They dazzle reason, as the Sun the eyes;
   And since I cannot fix on them my gaze
   Words must suffice that little speak their praise.

Rain from her beauty little flames of fire,
   Made living with a spirit to create
   Good thoughts, and crush the vices that innate
Make others vile. Fair one, who may desire
   Escape from blame as one not calm or meek,
   From her, who is God's thought, thy teaching seek.

My Song, it seems you speak this to oppose
   The saying of a sister Song of mine:
   This lowly Lady whom you call divine,
Your sister called disdainful and morose.
   Though Heaven, you know, is ever bright and pure,
   Eyes may have cause to find a star obscure.

So when your sister called this Lady proud
   She judged not truly, by what seemed; but fear
   Possessed her soul; and still, when I come near
Her glance, there's dread. Be such excuse allowed,
   My Song, and when thou canst, approach her, say;
   My Lady, take all homage I can pay.

CHAPTER I.

IN the preceding treatise is described how my second Love took its rise from the compassionate countenance of a Lady; which Love, finding my Soul inclined to its ardour, after the manner of fire, was kindled from a slight spark into a great flame; so that not only during my waking hours, but during sleep, its light threw many a vision into my mind. And how great the desire which Love excited to behold this Lady, it would be impossible either to tell or to make understood. And not only of her was I thus desirous, but of all those persons who had any nearness to her, either as acquaintances or as relations. Oh! how many were the nights, when the eyes of other persons were closed in sleep, that mine, wide open, gazed fixedly upon the tabernacle of my Love.

And as the rapidly increasing fire must of necessity be seen, it being impossible for fire to remain hidden, the desire seized me to speak of the Love that I could no longer restrain within me. And although I could receive but little help from my own counsel, yet, inasmuch as, either from the will of Love or from my own promptness, I drew nigh to it many times, I deliberated, and I saw that, in speaking of Love, there could be no more beautiful nor more profitable speech than that which commends the beloved person. And in this deliberation three reasons assisted me. One of them was self-love, which is the source of all the rest, as every one sees. For there is no more lawful nor more courteous way of doing honour to one's self than by doing honour to one's friend; and, since friendship cannot exist between the unlike, wherever one sees friendship, likeness is understood; and wherever likeness is understood, thither runs public praise or blame. And from this reason two great lessons may be learnt: the one is, never to wish that any vicious man should seem your friend, for in that case a bad opinion is formed of him who has made the evil man his friend; the other is, that no one ought to blame his friend publicly, because, if you consider well the aforesaid reason, he but points to himself with his finger in his eye.

The second reason was the desire for the duration of this friendship; wherefore it is to be known, as the Philosopher says in the ninth book of the Ethics, in the friendship of persons of unequal position it is requisite, for the preservation of that friendship, for a certain proportion to exist between them, which may reduce the dissimilarity to a similarity, as between the master and the servant. For, although the servant cannot render the same benefit to the master that is conferred on him, yet he ought to render the best that he can, with so much solicitude and free-will that that which is dissimilar in itself may become similar through the evidence of good-will, which proves the friendship, confirms and preserves it. Wherefore I, considering myself lower than that Lady, and perceiving myself benefited by her, endeavoured to praise her according to my ability. And, if it be not similar of itself, my prompt free-will proves at least that if I could I would do more, and thus it makes its friendship similar to that of this gentle Lady.

The third reason was an argument of prudence; for, as Boëthius says, "It is not sufficient to look only at that which is before the eyes, that is, at the Present; and, therefore, Prudence, Foresight, is given

to us, which looks beyond to that which may happen."
I say that I thought that for a long time I might
be reproached by many with levity of mind, on
hearing that I had turned from my first Love.
Wherefore, to remove this reproach, there was no
better argument than to state who the Lady was
who had thus changed me ; that, by her manifest
excellence, they might gain some perception of her
virtue ; and that, by the comprehension of her most
exalted virtue, they might be able to see that all
stability of mind could be in that mutability : and,
therefore, they should not judge me light and unstable. I then began to praise this Lady, and if not
in the most suitable manner, at least as well as I
could at first ; and I began to say : " Love, reasoning of my Lady in my mind." This Song chiefly
has three parts. The first is the whole of the first two
stanzas, in which I speak in a preliminary manner.
The second is the whole of the six following
stanzas, in which is described that which is intended,
i.e., the praise of that gentle Lady ; the first of which
begins : " The Sun sees not in travel round the
earth." The third part is in the last two stanzas, in
which, addressing myself to the Song, I purify it from
all doubtful interpretation. And these three parts
remain to be discussed now in due order.

CHAPTER II.

TURNING, then, to the First Part, which was composed as a Proem or Preface to the Song or Poem,
I say that it is fitly divided into three parts. In the
first place, it alludes to the ineffable condition of
this theme ; secondly, it describes my insufficiency

to speak of it in a perfect manner; and this second part begins: "If I would tell of her what thus I hear." Finally, I excuse myself for my insufficiency, for which they ought not to lay blame to my charge; and I commence this part when I say: "If my Song fail."

I begin, then: "Love, reasoning of my Lady in my mind," where in the first place it is to be seen who this speaker is, and what this place is in which I say that he is speaking. Love, taking him in his true sense, and considering him subtly, is no other than the spiritual union of the Soul with the beloved object; into which union, of its own nature, the Soul hastens sooner or later, according as it is free or impeded. And the reason for that natural disposition may be this: each substantial form proceeds from its First Cause, which is God, as is written in the book of Causes; and they receive not diversity from that First Cause, which is the most simple, but from the secondary causes, and from the material into which it descends. Wherefore, in the same book it is written, when treating of the infusion of the Divine Goodness: "The bounties and good gifts make diverse things, through the concurrence of that which receives them." Wherefore, since each effect retains somewhat of the nature of its cause, as Alfarabio says when he affirms that that which has been the first cause of a round body has in some way an essentially round form, so each form in some way has the essence of the Divine Nature in itself; not that the Divine Nature can be divided and communicated to these, but participated in by these, almost in the same way that the other stars participate in the nature of the Sun. And the nobler the form, the more does it retain of that Divine Nature.

Wherefore the human Soul, which is the noblest form of all those which are generated under Heaven, receives more from the Divine Nature than any other. And since it is most natural to wish to be in God, for as in the book quoted above one reads, the first thing is to exist, and before that there is nothing, the human Soul desires to exist naturally with all possible desire. And since its existence depends upon God, and is preserved by Him, it naturally desires and longs to be united to God, and so add strength to its own being. And since, in the goodness of Human Nature, Reason gives us proof of the Divine, it follows that, naturally, the Human Soul is united therewith by the path of the spirit so much the sooner, and so much the more firmly, in proportion as those good qualities appear more perfect; which appearance of perfection is achieved according as the power of the Soul to produce a good impression is strong and clear, or is trammelled and obscure. And this union is that which we call Love, whereby it is possible to know that which is within the Soul, by looking at those whom it loves in the world without. This Love, which is the union of my Soul with that gentle Lady in whom so much of the Divine Light was revealed to me, is that speaker of whom I speak; since from him continuous thoughts were born, whilst gazing at and considering the wondrous power of this Lady who was spiritually made one with my Soul.

The place in which I say that he thus speaks is the Mind. But in saying that it is the Mind, one does not attach more meaning to this than before; and therefore it is to be seen what this Mind properly signifies. I say, then, that the Philosopher, in the second book on the Soul, when speaking of its powers, says that the Soul principally has three powers, which are, to Live, to Feel, and to Reason: and he says also to Move, but it is possible to make this one with feeling, since every Soul moves that feels, either with all the senses or with one alone; for the power to move is conjoined with feeling. And according to that which he says, it is most evident that these powers are so entwined that the one is a foundation of the other; and that which is the foundation can of itself be divided; but the other, which is built upon it, cannot be apart from its foundation. Therefore, the Vegetative power, whereby one lives, is the foundation upon which one feels, that is, sees, hears, tastes, smells, and touches; and this vegetative power of itself can be the Soul, vegetative, as we see in all the plants. The Sensitive cannot exist without that. We find nothing that feels, and does not live. And this Sensitive power is the foundation of the Intellectual, that is, of the Reason; so that, in animate mortals, the Reasoning power is not found without the Sensitive. But the Sensitive is found without Reason, as in the beasts, and in the birds, and in the fishes, and in any brute animal, as we see. And that Soul which contains all these powers is the most perfect of all. And the Human Soul possessing the nobility of the highest power, which is Reason, participates in the Divine Nature, after the manner of an eternal Intelligence: for the Soul is ennobled and denuded of matter by that Sovereign Power in proportion as the Divine Light of Truth shines into it, as into an Angel; and Man is therefore called by the Philosophers the Divine Animal.

In this most noble part of the Soul are many virtues, as the Philosopher says, especially in the third chapter of the Soul, where he says that there is in it a virtue which is called Scientific, and one which is called Ratiocinative, or rather deliberative ; and with this there are certain virtues, as Aristotle says in that same place, such as the Inventive and the Judging. And all these most noble virtues, and the others which are in that excellent power, are designated by that one word, which we sought to understand, that is, Mind. Wherefore it is evident that by Mind is meant the highest, noblest part of a man's Soul.

And it is seen to be so, for only of man and of the Divine substances is this Mind predicated, as can plainly be seen in Boëthius, who first predicates it of men, where he says to Philosophy: "Thou, and God who placed thee in the mind of men ;" then he predicates it of God, when he says: "Thou dost produce everything from the Divine Model, Thou most beautiful One, bearing the beautiful World in Thy mind." Neither was it ever predicated of brute animals ; nay, of many men who appear defective in the most perfect part, it does not seem that it ought to be, or that it could be, predicated ; and therefore such as these are termed in the Latin Tongue *amenti* and *dementi*, that is, without mind. Hence one can now perceive that it is Mind which is the perfect and most precious part of the Soul in which is God.

And that is the place where I say that Love discourses to me of my Lady.

CHAPTER III.

NOT without cause do I say that this Love was at work in my mind; but it is said reasonably, in order to explain what this Love is, by the place in which it works. Wherefore, it is to be known that each thing, as is said above, for the reason shown above, has its especial Love, as the simple bodies have Love innate, each in its proper place. Therefore the Earth always descends to the centre, the fire to the circumference above near the Heaven of the Moon, and always ascends towards that. The bodies first composed, such as are the minerals, have love for the place where their generation is ordained, and in which they increase, and from which they have vigour and power. Wherefore, we see the loadstone always receive power from the place of its generation. Each of the plants which are first animated, that is, first animated with a vegetative soul has most evident love for a particular place, according as its nature may require; and therefore we see certain plants almost always grow by the side of the streams, and certain others upon the mountain tops, and certain others grow by the sea-shore, or at the foot of hills, which, if they are transplanted, either die entirely or live a sad life, as it were, like a being separated from his friend. The brute beasts have a most evident love, not only for places, but we see also their love towards each other. Men have their own love for things perfect and excellent; and since Man, although his Soul is one substance alone, because of his nobility, partakes of the nature of each of these things, he can possess all these affections, and he does possess them all. By his part in the nature of the simple body, as earth, naturally it tends downwards; therefore, when he moves his body upwards, he becomes more weary.

Because of the second nature, of the mixed body, it loves the place of its generation, and even the time; and therefore each one naturally is of more power in his own place and in his own time than in any other. Wherefore, one reads in the History of Hercules, and in the greater Ovid, and in Lucan, and in other Poets, that when fighting with the Giant who was named Antæus, every time that the Giant was weary, and laid his body down on the earth at full length, either by the will or strength of Hercules, new strength and vigour then surged up in him, drawn wholly from the Earth, in which and from which he was produced; Hercules, perceiving this, at last seized him, and having compressed and raised him above the Earth, he held him so tightly, without allowing him to touch the Earth again, that he conquered Antæus by excess of strength, and killed him. According to the testimony of the books, this battle took place in Africa.

And because of the third nature, that is, of the plants, Man has a love for a certain food, not inasmuch as it affects the senses, but in so much as it is nutritious; and that particular food does the work of that most perfect Nature, while certain other food, dissimilar, acts but imperfectly. And therefore we see that certain food will make men handsome, and strong-limbed, and very brightly coloured, and certain other food will do the opposite of this.

And by the fourth nature, of the animals, that is, the sensitive, Man has the other love, by which he loves according to the sensible appearance, like the beasts; and this love in Man especially has need of control, because of its excessive operation in the delights given, especially through sight and touch.

And because of the fifth and last nature, which is the true Human Nature, and, to use a better phrase, the Angelic, namely, the Rational, Man has by it the Love of Truth and Virtue; and from this Love is born true and perfect friendship from the honest intercourse of which the Philosopher speaks in the eighth book of the Ethics, when he treats of Friendship.

Wherefore, since this nature is termed Mind, as is proved above, I spoke of Love as discoursing in my Mind in order to explain that this Love was the Friendship which is born of that most noble nature, that is, of Truth and Virtue, and to exclude each false opinion, by which my Love might be suspected to spring from pleasure of the Senses.

I then say, "With constant pleasure," to make people understand its continuance and its fervour. And I say that it often whispers "Things over which the intellect may stray." And I speak truth, because my thoughts, when reasoning of her, often sought to draw conclusions of her, which I could not comprehend, and I was alarmed, so that I seemed almost like one dazed, even as he who, looking with the eye along a direct line, sees first the nearest things clearly; then, proceeding, it sees them less clearly; then, further on, doubtfully; then, proceeding an immense way, the sight is divided from the object, and sees nothing. And this is one unspeakable thing of that which I have taken for a theme; and consequently I relate the other when I say:

> His words make music of so sweet a kind
> That the Soul hears and feels, and cries, Ah, me,
> That I want power to tell what thus I see!

And because I know not how to tell it, I say that my soul laments, saying, "Ah, me, that I want power." And this is the other unspeakable thing, that the tongue is not a complete and perfect follower of all that the intellect sees. And I say, "That the Soul hears and feels;" hearing, as to the words, and feeling, as to the sweetness of the sound.

CHAPTER IV.

Now that the two ineffable parts of this matter have been discussed, we must proceed to discuss words that describe my insufficiency.

I say, then, that my insufficiency arises from a double cause, even as in a twofold manner the exalted nature of my Lady surpasses all, in the way which has been told. For I am compelled, by the poverty of my intellect, to omit much of the truth concerning her which shone into my mind like rays of light, but which my mind receives like a transparent body, unable to gather up the ends thereof and reflect them back. And this I express in that following part: "First, all that Reason cannot make its own I needs must leave." Then, when I say, "And of what can be known," I say that not even to that which I do understand am I sufficient, because my tongue is not so eloquent that it could tell that which is discoursed in my thoughts concerning her. It may be seen, therefore, that, with respect to the Truth, it is very little that I shall say; and this redounds to her great praise, if well considered, in that which was the main intention. And it is possible to say that this form of speech came indeed from the workshop of Rhetoric, which on every side lays its hand upon the main intention. Then, when it says, "If my Song fail," I excuse myself for my fault, which ought not, then, to be blamed when others see that my words are far below the dignity of this Lady. And I say that, if the defect is in my rhymes, that is, in my words, which are appointed to discourse of her, for this are to be blamed the weakness of the intellect and the abruptness of our speech: "blame wit and words," which are overpowered by the thought, so that they cannot follow it entirely, especially there where the thought is born of love, because there the Soul searches more deeply than elsewhere. It would be quite possible for any one to say: Thou dost excuse and accuse thyself all in one breath, which is a reason for blame, not for escape from blame, inasmuch as the blame, which is mine, is cast on the intellect and on the speech; for, if it be good, I ought to be praised for it in so much as it is so; and if it be defective, I ought to be blamed. To this it is possible to reply, briefly, that I do not accuse myself, but that I excuse myself in truth. And therefore it is to be known, according to the opinion of the Philosopher in the third book of the Ethics, that man is worthy of praise or of blame only in those things which it is in his power to do or not to do; but in those things over which he has no power he deserves neither blame nor praise, since either the praise or blame is to be attributed to some other, although the things may be parts of the man himself. Therefore, we ought not to blame the man because his body, from his birth, may be ugly, since it was not in his power to make it beautiful; but our blame should fall on the evil disposition of the matter whereof he is made, whose source was a defect of Nature. And even so we ought not to praise the man for the beauty of form which he may have from his birth, for he was not the maker of it; but we ought to praise the artificer, that is, Human Nature, who shapes her material into so much beauty when she is not impeded. And therefore the priest said well to the Emperor who laughed and scoffed at the ugliness of his body: "The Lord, He is God: It is He that hath made us, and not we ourselves;" and these are the words of the Prophet in a verse of the Psalms, written neither more nor less than according to the reply of the Priest.

And therefore let the wicked evil-born ones perceive that, if they put their chief care in the adornment of their persons, it must be with all modesty; for to do that is no other than to adorn the work of another, that is, Nature, and to abandon their own proper work.

Returning, then, to the proposition, I say that our intellect, through defect of the power through which it sees organic power, that is, the imagination, is not able to ascend to certain things, because the imagination cannot help it and has not the wherewithal, such as are the substances apart from matter, which (if we can have any knowledge of them) we cannot fully comprehend.

And the man is not to blame for this, because he was not the maker of this defect; nay, Universal Nature did this, which is God, who wills that in this life we be without this light. And because He was the cause, it would be presumptuous to argue concerning it. So that if my earnest thought transported me into a place where my imagination failed my intellect, I was not to blame if I could not possibly understand.

Again, a bound is set to our understanding in each operation thereof; but not by us, but by Universal Nature; and therefore it is to be known that the bounds of the understanding are wider in thought than in speech, and wider in speech than in signs. Hence, if our thought, not only that which fails in a perfect intellect, but also that which in a perfect intellect attains its end, is the conqueror of speech, we are not to blame, because we are not the makers of it. And therefore I prove that I do truthfnlly excuse myself when I say: "Blame wit and words, whose force Fails to tell all that I hear Love discourse;" for, sufficiently clear ought to appear the good-will, which alone we should regard in respect to merits that are human.

And thus is now explained the first principal part of this Song which flows from my hand.

CHAPTER V.

DISCOURSE on the first part of the Song has now made its meaning open and clear, and it is needful to proceed to the second; for the clearer perception of which, three divisions are desirable, according as it is contained in three sections. For in the first part I praise that Lady entirely and generally, as in the Soul so in the body; in the second part I descend to especial commendation of the Soul; and in the third, to especial praise of the body. The first part begins: "The Sun sees not in travel round the earth;" the second begins: "Her Maker saw that she was good;" the third begins: "Rain from her beauty little flames of fire;" and these parts or divisions in due order are to be discussed.

I say then: "The Sun sees not in travel round the earth;" where it is to be known, in order to have perfect understanding thereof, how the Earth is circled round by the Sun. In the first place, I say that by the Earth I do not here mean the whole body of the Universe, but only that part of the sea and land, following the common speech, which is thus wont to designate it, whereupon some one exclaims, "This man has seen all the World," meaning "this part of the sea and land." This World Pythagoras and his followers asserted to be one of the stars, and they also said that there was another opposite to it, similar to it: and they called that one Antictona; and he said that both were in one sphere which revolved from East to West, and by this revolution the Sun was circled round us, and now he was seen, and now he was not seen. And he said that the fire was in the centre of these, considering the fire to be a more noble body than the water and than the Earth, and giving the noblest centre to the four simple bodies; he said that the fire, when it appeared to ascend, according to strict truth descended to the centre. Then Plato was of another opinion, and he wrote in a book of his, which he called Timæus, that the Earth with the sea was indeed the centre of all, but that its whole sphere revolved round its centre, following the first movement of the Heavens, but much slower on account of its gross material, and because of the immense distance from that first moved. These opinions are confuted in the second chapter, Of Heaven and the World, by that glorious Philosopher, to whom Nature opened her secrets most freely; and by him it is therein proved that this

World, the Earth, is of itself stable and fixed to all eternity. And his reasons, which Aristotle states in order to break those other opinions and to affirm the truth, it is not my intention here to narrate; therefore, let it be enough for those to whom I speak, to know, upon his great authority, that this Earth is fixed, and does not revolve, and that it, with the sea, is the centre of the Heavens. These Heavens revolve round this centre continuously, even as we see; in which revolution there must of necessity be two fixed Poles, and a circle equally distant from these round which all especially revolves. Of these two Poles, the one is visible to almost all the discovered Earth, that is, the Northern Pole; the other is hidden from almost all the discovered Earth, that is, the Southern Pole. The circle spread from them is that part of Heaven under which the Sun revolves when it is in Aries and Libra. Wherefore, it is to be known that if a stone could fall from this Pole of ours, it would fall there beyond into the sea precisely upon that surface of the sea, where, if a man could be, he would always have the Sun above the middle of his head; and I believe that from Rome to that place, going in a straight line to the North, the distance may be almost two thousand seven hundred miles, or a little more or less. Imagining, then, in order to understand better what I say, that there is in that place a city, and that its name may be Maria, I say again that if from the other Pole, that is, the Southern, a stone could fall, that it would fall upon that part of the ocean which is precisely on this ball opposite to Maria; and I believe that from Rome to where this second stone would fall, going in a direct line to the South, the distance may be seven thousand five hundred miles, a little more or less. And here let us imagine another city, which may have the name of Lucia; and the distance, from whatever part one draws the line, is ten thousand two hundred miles between the one and the other, that is, half the circumference of this ball, so that the citizens of Maria hold the soles of the feet opposite the soles of the feet of the citizens of Lucia. Let us imagine also a circle upon this ball which is in every part equi-distant from Maria as from Lucia. I believe that this circle, according to what I understand by the assertions of the Astrologers, and by that of Albertus Magnus in his book On the Nature of Places and on the Properties of the Elements, and also by the testimony of Lucan in his ninth book, would divide this Earth uncovered by the sea in the Meridian, almost through all the extreme end of the first climate, where there are amongst the other people the Garamanti, who are almost always naked; to whom came Cato with the people of Rome when flying from the dominion of Cæsar. Having marked out these three places upon this ball, one can easily see how the Sun circles round it.

I say, then, that the Heaven of the Sun revolves from West to East, not directly against the diurnal movement, that is, of the day and night, but obliquely against that, so that its mid-circle, which is equally between its Poles, in which is the body of the Sun, cuts into two opposite parts the circle of the two first Poles, in the beginning of Aries and in the beginning of Libra; and it is divided by two arcs from it, one towards the North and one towards the South; the points of these two said arcs are equi-distant from the first circle in every part by twenty-three degrees and one point more, and the one point is the tropic of Cancer, and the other is the tropic of Capricorn ; therefore it must be that Maria in the sign of Aries can see, when the Sun sinks below the mid-circle of the first Poles, this Sun to revolve round the Earth below, or rather the sea, like a millstone, of which only one half of its body appears, and can see this come rising up after the manner of the screw of a vine-press, so much so that it completes ninety-one rotations, or a little more. When these rotations are completed, its ascension is to Maria almost as much in proportion as it ascends to us in the half-third, that is, of the equal day and night ; and if a man could stand in Maria, with his face always turned to the Sun, he would see that Sun pass by on the right. Then by the same way it seems to descend another ninety-one rotations, or a little more, so much so that it circles round below the Earth, or rather sea, not showing the whole of itself ; and then it is hidden, and Lucia begins to see it, which, the same as Maria, then sees it to ascend and to descend around itself with the same number of rotations. And if a man could stand in Lucia, with his face always turned towards the Sun, he would see it pass to the left. Therefore, it is possible to see that these places have in the year one day of six months' duration, and one night of the same length of time ; and when one has the day the other has the night.

It must be also that the circle where the Garamanti are, as has been said above, upon this ball, can see the Sun revolve precisely above them, not after the fashion of a mill-stone, but of a wheel, which cannot in any part be seen except the centre, when it goes under Aries. And then it is seen to depart from its place immediately above and go towards Maria ninety-one days, or a little more, and by so many to return to its position ; and then, when it has turned back, it goes before Libra, and even so departs and goes towards Lucia ninety-one days, or a little more, and in so many returns to its position. And this place always has the day equal with the night, either on this side or on that, as the Sun goes, and twice a year it has the summer of intense heat, and two little winters. It must also be that the two distances, which are midway from the two imaginary Cities and the mid-circle, see the Sun variously, according as they are remote from, and near to, these places.

Now, by what has been said, this can be seen by him who has good understanding, to which it is well to give a little fatigue. He can now perceive that, by the Divine Providence, the World is so ordained that the sphere of the Sun, being revolved and turned round to one point, this ball whereon we are in every part receives an equal share of light and darkness. Oh, ineffable Wisdom, Thou which didst thus ordain ! Oh, how poor and feeble is our mind when seeking to comprehend Thee ! And you, O men, for whose benefit and pleasure I write, in what fearful blindness do you live if you never raise your eyes upwards to these things, but keep them fixed in the mud of your foolishness.

CHAPTER VI.

IN the preceding chapter is shown after what manner the Sun travels round the Earth ; so that now one can proceed to demonstrate the meaning of the part to which this thought belongs. I say, then, that in that first part I begin to praise that Lady by comparison with other things. And I say that the Sun, circling round the Earth, sees nothing so gentle as that Lady; wherefore it follows that she is, according to the letter, the most gentle of all things that the sun shines upon. And it says: "Till the hour;" wherefore it is to be known that "hour" is understood in two ways by the Astrologers. The one is, that of the day and of the night they make twenty-four hours—twelve of the day, twelve of the night, however long or short the day may be. And these hours are short and long in the day and night according as the day and night increase and diminish. And these hours the Church uses when it says, Prima, Tertia, Sexta, and Nona—first, third, sixth, and ninth; and these are termed hours temporal. The other mode is, that, making of the day and of the night twenty-four hours, the day sometimes has fifteen hours and the night nine; and sometimes the night has sixteen and the day eight, according as the day and night increase and diminish; and they term these hours equal at the Equinox, and those that are termed temporal are always the same, because, the day being equal to the night, it must happen thus.

Then when I say, "All Minds of Heaven wonder at her worth," I praise her, not having respect to any other thing. And I say that the Intelligences of Heaven behold her, and that the people here below think of that gentle Lady when they have more of that peace which delights them. And here it is to be known that each Mind or Intellect in Heaven above, according to that which is written in the book Of Causes, knows that which is above itself and that which is below itself; therefore it knows God as its

Cause; therefore it knows that which is below itself as its effect.

And since God is the most universal cause of everything, to know Him is to know all, according to the degree of the Intelligence; wherefore all the Intelligences know the human form in as far as it is by intention fixed or determined in the Divine Mind. The moving Intelligences especially know it; since they are the most especial causes of it, and of every kind of form; and they know the most perfect, as far as they can know it, as their rule and pattern.

And if this human form, copied and individualized, is not perfect, it is not the fault of the said copy or image, but of the matter from which the individual is formed. Therefore when I say, "All Minds in Heaven wonder at her worth," I wish to express no other than that she is thus made, even as the express image of the human form in the Divine Mind. And each Mind there above beholds her by virtue of that quality which exists especially in those angelic Minds which build up and shape, with Heaven, things that exist below. And to confirm this, I subjoin when I say, "Mortals, enamoured, find her in their thought When Love his peace into their minds has brought," where it is to be known that each thing especially desires its perfection, and in that its every desire finds peace and calm, and for that peace each thing is desired.

And this is that desire which always makes every pleasure appear incomplete, for there is no joy or pleasure so great in this life that it can quench the thirst in our Soul, for always the desire for that perfection remains in the Mind. And since this Lady is truly that perfection, I say that people here below receive great delight when they have most peace; for she abides then in their thoughts. For this Lady, I say, is perfect in as high a degree as it is possible for Human Nature to be.

Then when I say, "Her Maker saw that she was good," I prove that not only this Lady is the most perfect in the human race, but more than the most perfect, inasmuch as she receives from the Divine Goodness more than human dues. Wherefore one can reasonably believe that as each Master loves most his best work far more than the other work, so God loves the good human being far above the rest. And forasmuch as His Bounty is of necessity not restricted by any limit, His love has no regard to the amount due to him who receives, but it overflows in gifts, and in the blessings of power and grace. Wherefore I say here, that this God, who gave life or being to this Lady, through love or charity for her perfection pours into her of His Bounty beyond the limits of the amount due to our nature.

Then when I say, "On her pure soul," I prove this that has been said with reasonable testimony, which gives us to know that, as the Philosopher says in the second chapter, On the Soul, the Soul is the act of the Body; and if it be its act, it is its Cause; and as it is written in the book before quoted, On Causes, each Cause infuses into its effect some of the goodness which it receives from its own Cause, which is "God." Wherefore, since in her are seen wonderful things, so much so on the part of the body that they make each beholder desirous to see those things, it is evident that her form, which is her Soul, guides it as its proper Cause and receives miraculously the gracious goodness of God.

And thus is proved, by that appearance, which exceeds the due appointment of our nature, which in her is most perfect, as has been said above, that this Lady is by God endowed with good gifts and made a noble thing. And this is the whole Literal meaning of the first section of the second principal part.

CHAPTER VII.

HAVING commended this Lady generally, both according to the Soul and according to the Body, I proceed to praise her specially according to the Soul.

And first I praise her Soul for its goodness, that is great in itself; then I commend it for a goodness that is great in others, and useful to the World. And that second part begins when I say, firstly, "On her fair frame Virtue Divine descends;" where it is to be known that the Divine Goodness descends into all things, and otherwise they could not exist; but, although this goodness springs from the First Cause, it is received diversely, according to the more or less of virtue in the recipients. Wherefore it is written in the book Of Causes: "The First Goodness sends His good gifts forth upon things in one stream. Verily each thing receives from this stream according to the manner of its virtue and its being." And we can have a sensible, living example of this in the Sun. We see the light of the Sun, which is one thing, derived from one fountain, to be variously received by material substances; as Albertus Magnus says in his book On the Intellect, that certain bodies, through having mixed in themselves an excess of transparent brightness, so soon as the Sun sees them they become so bright that, by the multiplication of light within them, their aspect is hardly discernible, and from themselves they render back to others great splendour or brilliancy, such as is gold and any gem. Sure I am that by being entirely transparent, not only do they receive the light, but that they do not intercept it ; nay, they pass it on, like stained glass, coloured with their own colour, to other things. And there are certain other bodies so overpowering in the purity of the transparency that they become so radiant as to overpower the adjustments of the eye, and you cannot look at them without fatigue of sight; such as are the mirrors. Certain others are so free from transparency, that but little light can they receive ; as is the Earth. Thus the Goodness of God is received in sundrywise by the sundry substances, that is, in one way by the Angels, who are without grossness of matter, as if transparent through their purity of form ; and otherwise by the human Soul, which although on one side it may be free from matter, on another side it is impeded : even as the man who is all in the water but his head, of whom one cannot say that he is entirely in the water, or entirely out of it. Again otherwise it is received by the animals, whose soul is wholly comprised in matter ; but I say that the soul of animals receives of the Goodness of God in proportion as it is ennobled. Again otherwise is it received by the minerals ; and otherwise by the Earth, than by the others, because the Earth is most material, and therefore most remote, and most out of all proportion to the First most simple and most high Cause, which is alone Intellectual, that is to say, God.

And although here below there may be placed general degrees of excellence, nevertheless, singular degrees of excellence may also be placed; that is to say, that amongst human Souls one Soul may receive more bountifully than another. And since in the intellectual order of the Universe one ascends and descends by degrees almost continuous from the lowest form to the highest, and from the highest to the lowest, as we see in the visible order of things; and between the Angelic Nature, which is intellectual, and the Human Soul there may be no step, but the one rise to the other as it were continuously through the height of the degrees; and from the Human Soul and the most perfect soul of the brute animals, again, there may not be any break in the descent. For as we see many men so vile and of such low condition that it seems almost that it can be no other than bestial, so it is to be asserted and firmly believed that there may be some men so noble and of a condition so exalted that it can be no other than that of the Angel Otherwise the human species could not be continued on every side, which cannot be. Such as these Aristotle calls, in the seventh book of the Ethics, Divine; and such a one I say that this Lady is, so that the Divine Virtue, after the manner that it descends into the Angel, descends into her.

Then when I say, "Fair one who doubt," I prove this by the experience that it is possible to have of it in those operations which are proper to the rational Soul, wherein the Divine Light shines forth more quickly, that is, in the speech and in the actions, which are woht to be termed conduct and deportment. Wherefore it is to be known that only man amongst the animals speaks, and has conduct and acts which are called rational, because he alone has Reason in himself. And if any one might wish to say, in contradiction, that a certain bird can speak, as appears true, especially of the magpie and of the parrot; and that some beast performs acts, or rather things, by rule, as appears in the ape and in some other; I reply that it is not true that they speak, nor that they have rules, because they have not Reason, from which these things must proceed; neither is there in them the principle of these operations; neither do they know what that is; neither do they understand that by those acts something is intended; but that only which they see and hear they represent, even as the image of somebody may be reflected in a glass. Wherefore, as in the mirror the corporal image which the mirror shows is not true, so the image of Reason, in the acts and the speech which the brute soul represents, or rather shows, is not true. I say that what gentle Lady soever doubts should "go with her, mark the grace In all her acts." I do not say man, because one can derive experience more modestly from the woman than from the man; and I say she will find that "Downward from Heaven bends An angel when she speaks." For her speech, because of its exalted character and because of its sweetness, kindles in the mind of him who hears it a thought of Love, which I call a celestial Spirit; since from Heaven is the source and from Heaven the intention thereof, as has been already narrated. From which thought I pass to a firm opinion that this Lady is of miraculous power, that there is "A power in her by none of us possessed." Her actions, by their suavity and by their moderation, "Rival in calls to Love that Love must hear."

They cause Love to awaken and again to hear whenever he is sown by the power of bountiful Nature. Which natural seed acts as in the next treatise is shown.

Then when I say, "Fair in all like her, fairest she'll appear Who is most like her," I intend to narrate how the goodness and the power of her soul are good and useful to others; and, firstly, how useful it is to other women, saying that she is "Fair in all like her," where I present a clear or bright example to the women, from gazing at which they can make their beauty seem gentle in following the same. Secondly, I relate how useful she is to all people, saying that her aspect assists our faith, which is more useful to the whole Human Race than all other things beside; for it is that by which we escape from Eternal Death and acquire Eternal Life; and she assists our Faith, for the first foundation of our Faith is on the miracles performed by Him who was crucified, who created our Reason, and willed that it should be less than His power. He performed these miracles, then, in His own name for His saints; and many men are so obstinate that they are in doubt of those miracles if there be the least mist or cloud around them; and they cannot believe any miracle unless they have visible experience of the same; and this Lady is a thing visibly miraculous, of which the eyes of men daily can have experience, and which can make the other miracles appear possible to us. Wherefore it is manifest that this Lady, with her marvellous aspect, assists our Faith. And, therefore, finally I say:

> We, content to call
> Her face a Miracle, have Faith made sure:
> For that God made her ever to endure.

And thus ends the second section of the second principal part of the Song according to its Literal meaning.

CHAPTER VIII.

AMONGST the Works of Divine Wisdom, Man is the most wonderful, considering how in one form the Divine Power joined three natures; and in such a form how subtly harmonized his body must be. It is organized for all his distinct powers; wherefore, because of the great concord there must be, among so many organs, to secure their perfect response to each other, in all the multitude of men but few are perfect. And if this Creature is so wonderful, certainly it is a dread thing to discourse of his conditions, not only in words, but even in thought. So that to this apply those words of Ecclesiastes: "I beheld all the Work of God, that a Man cannot find out the Work that is done under the Sun." And those other words there, where he says: "Let not thine heart be hasty to utter anything before God: for God is in Heaven, and thou upon Earth: therefore let thy words be few." I, then, who in this third section intend to speak of a certain condition of such a creature, inasmuch as, through the goodness of the Soul, visible beauty appears in his body, I begin timorously uncertain, intending, if not fully, at least partially, to untie such a knot as this. I say, then, that since the meaning of that section is clear, wherein this Lady is praised on the part of the Soul, we are now to proceed and to see how it is when I say: "Her aspect shows delights of Paradise."

I praise her on the part of the body, and I say that in her aspect bright gleams appear which show us pleasant things, and amongst others those of Paradise.

The most noble state of all, and that which is the crown of every good, is to be at peace within one's self; and this is to be happy. And this content is truly (although in another manner) in her aspect; so that, by looking at her, the people find peace, so sweetly does her Beauty feed the eyes of the beholders; but in another way, for the Peace that is perpetual in Paradise is not attainable by any man.

And since some one might ask where this wonderful content appears in this Lady, I distinguish in her person two parts, in which human pleasure and displeasure most appear. Wherefore it is to be known that in whatever part the Soul most fulfils its office, it strives most earnestly to adorn that part, and there it does its work most subtly. Wherefore we see that in the Face of Man, where it fulfils its office more than in any other outward part, it works so subtly that, by making itself subtle therein as much as its material permits, it causes that no face is like another, because its utmost power over matter, which is dissimilar in almost all, is there brought into action; and because in the face the Soul works especially in two places, as if in those two places all the three Natures of the Soul had jurisdiction, that is, in the Eyes and in the Mouth, these it chiefly adorns, and there it spends its care to make all beautiful if it can. And in these two places I say that those pleasures of content appear, saying: "Seen in her eyes and in her smiling face;" the which two places, by means of a beautiful comparison, may be designated the balconies of the woman who dwells in the house of the body, she being the Soul; because there, although veiled, as it were, the Soul often shows itself. The Soul shows itself so evidently in the eyes that it is possible to know its present passion if you look attentively.

Six passions are proper to the human Soul of which the Philosopher makes mention in his Rhetoric, namely, Grace, Zeal, Mercy, Envy, Love, and Shame; and with whichever of these the Soul is impassioned, there comes into the window of the Eyes the semblance of it, unless it be repressed within, and shut from view by great power of will. Wherefore some one formerly plucked out his eyes that an inward shame should not appear without, as Statius the Poet says of the Theban Œdipus when he says that with eternal night he loosed his damnèd shame.

It reveals itself in the Mouth, like colour behind glass as it were. And what is a smile or a laugh except a coruscation of the Soul's delight, a light shot outwardly from that which shines within? And therefore it is right for a man to reveal his Soul by a well-tempered cheerfulness, smiling moderately with a due restraint, and with slight movement of the limbs; so that the Lady, that is, the Soul, which then, as has been said, shows herself, may appear modest, and not dissolute. Therefore the book on the Four Cardinal Virtues commands us thus: "Let thy smile be without loud laughter, that is, without cackling like a hen."

Ah, the sweet wonder of my Lady's smile, which is never seen but in the eyes!

And I say of these delights seen in her eyes and smile: "Love brought them there as to his dwelling place;" where it is possible to consider Love in a twofold form. First, the Love of the Soul, peculiar or proper to these places; secondly, universal Love, which inclines things to love and to be loved, which ordains the Soul to rule these parts.

Then, when I say, "They dazzle Reason," I excuse myself for this, that it appears of such exceeding beauty that I can tell but little, owing to its overpowering force; and I say that I can say but little concerning it for two reasons. The one is, that those things which appear in her aspect overpower our intellect; and I tell how this conquest is made: that "They dazzle Reason, as sunbeams our eyes," when the Sun overpowers our feeble sight, if not also the healthy and the strong. The other is, that the man cannot look fixedly at it, because the Soul becomes inebriate therein; so that incontinently, after gazing thereat, it fails in all its operations.

Then, when I say, "Rain from her beauty little flames of fire," I recur to discourse of its effect, since to discourse entirely of it is not possible. Wherefore it is to be known that all those things which subdue our intellect, so that it is unable to see what they are, are most suitably to be discussed in their effects; wherefore of God, and of His separate substances, and of the first matter we can thus have some knowledge. And therefore I say that the beauty of that Lady rains little flames of fire, meaning the ardour of Love and of Charity, "Made living with a spirit," that is, Love informed by a gentle spirit, which is direct desire, through which and from which "to create Good thoughts;" and it not only does this, but it crushes and destroys its opposite, the innate vices which are especially the foes of all good thoughts.

And here it is to be known that there are certain vices in the Man to which he is naturally disposed; as certain men of a choleric complexion are disposed to anger: and such vices as these are innate, that is, natural. Others are the vices of habit, for which not the complexion, but habit, or custom, is to blame; such as intemperance, and especially intemperance in wine. But these vices are subdued and put to flight by good habits, and the man is made virtuous thereby without finding fatigue in his moderation, as the Philosopher says in the second book of the Ethics. Truly there is this difference between the natural passions and the habitual, that through use of good morals the habitual entirely vanish, because their origin, the evil habit, is destroyed by its opposite; but the natural, the source of which is in the complexion of the passionate man, although they may be made much lighter by good morals, yet they do not entirely disappear as far as regards the first cause, but they almost wholly disappear in act, because custom is not equal to nature, which is the source of such a passion. And therefore the man is more praiseworthy who guides himself and rules himself when he is of an evil disposition by nature, in opposition to natural impulse, than he who, being gifted with a good disposition by nature, carries himself naturally well; as it is more praiseworthy to control a bad horse than one that is not troublesome. I say, then, that those little flames which rain down from her beauty destroy the innate, or the natural, vices, to make men understand that her beauty has power to renew Nature in those who behold it, which is a miraculous thing. And this confirms that which is observed above in the other chapter when I say that she is the helper of our Faith.

Finally, when I say, "Lady, who may desire Escape from blame," I infer, under pretext of admonishing another, the end for which so much beauty was made. And I say that what lady believes her beauty to be open to blame through some defect, let her look on this most perfect example; where it is understood that it is designed not only to improve and raise the good, but also to convert evil to good. And, finally, it is subjoined that she is "God's thought," that is, from the Mind of God. And this to make men understand that, by design of the Creator, Nature is made to produce such an effect.

And thus ends the whole of the second chief part of the Song.

CHAPTER IX.

THE order of the present treatise requires, after these two parts of the Song have been discussed, according to my intention, that we now proceed to the third, in which I intend to purify the Song from a reproof which might be unfavourable to it.

And it is this, that before I composed it, this Lady seeming to me to be somewhat fierce and haughty against me, I made a little ballad, in which I called her proud and angry, which appears to be contrary to that which is here reasoned; and therefore I turn to the Song, and, under colour of teaching it how it is proper that it should excuse itself, I make an excuse for that which came before. And this, when one addresses inanimate things, is a figure which is called by rhetoricians, Prosopopœia, and the Poets often use it. "My Song, it seems you speak this to oppose." The intention of which address, to make it more easy of understanding, it behoves me to divide into three sections: first, one affirms wherefore excuse is necessary; then, one proceeds with the excuse, when I say, "Though Heaven, you know;" finally, I speak to the Song as to a person well skilled in that which it is right to do when I say, "Be such excuse allowed."

I say, then, in the first place: "My Song, it seems you speak this to oppose The saying of a sister Song of mine." For the sake of similitude, I say sister; for as that woman is called a sister who is born of the same father, so may a man call that work a sister which is wrought by the same worker; for our work is in some degree a thing begotten. And I say why it seems opposed or contrary to that sister Song, saying: "This lovely Lady whom you count divine, Your sister called disdainful and morose." This accusation being affirmed, I proceed to the excuse, by quoting an example, wherein the Truth is quite opposite to the appearance of Truth, and it is quite possible to take the false semblance of Truth for Truth itself, regarding Truth itself as Falsehood. I say: "Though Heaven, you know, is ever high and pure, Men's eyes may fail, and find a star obscure;" where it is shown that it is the property of colour and light to be visible, as Aristotle affirms in the second book Of the Soul and in the book on Sense and Sensation. Other things, indeed, are visible, but it is not their property to be so, nor to be tangible, as in form, height, number, motion, and rest, which are said to be subject to the Common Sense, and which we comprehend by union of many senses; but of colour and light it is the property to be visible, because with the sight only we comprehend them. These visible things, both those of which it is the property and those subject to the Common Sense, inasmuch as they are visible, come within the eye; I do not say the things, but their form; through the transparent medium, not really, but by intention, as it were through transparent glass. And in the humour which is in the pupil of the eye this current which makes the form visible is completed, because that humour is closed behind like a mirror which has its glass backed with lead; so that it cannot pass farther on, but strikes there, after the manner of a ball, and stops; so that the form which does not appear in the transparent medium, having reached the disc behind, shines brightly thereon; and this is the reason why the image appears only in the glass which has lead at the back.

From this pupil the visual spirit, which is continued from it to the part of the Brain, the anterior, where the sensitive power is, suddenly, without loss of time, depicts it as in the clear spring of a fountain; and thus we see. Wherefore, in order that its vision be truthful, that is, such as the visible thing is in itself, the medium through which the form comes to the eye must be without any colour, and so also the humour of the pupil; otherwise the visible form would be stained of the colour of the medium and of that of the pupil. And this is the reason why they who wish to make things appear of a certain colour in a mirror interpose that colour between the glass and the lead, the glass being pressed over it.

Plato and other Philosophers said, indeed, that our sight was not because the visible came into the eye, but because the visual virtue went out to the visible form. And this opinion is confuted by the Philosopher in that book of his on Sense and Sensation. Having thus considered this law of vision, one can easily perceive how, although the star is always in one way bright, clear, and resplendent, and receives no change whatever except that of local movement, as is proved in that book on Heaven and the World, yet from many causes it may appear dim and obscure; since it may appear thus on account of the medium, the atmosphere, that changes continually. This medium changes from light to darkness, according to the presence or absence of the Sun; and during the presence of the Sun the medium, which is transparent, is so full of light that it overpowers the star, and therefore it no longer appears brilliant. This medium also changes from rare to dense, from dry to moist, because of the vapours of the Earth which rise continually. The medium, thus changed, changes by its density the image of the star, which passes through it, makes it appear dim, and by its moisture or dryness changes it in colour. In like manner it may thus appear through the visual organ, that is, the eye, which on account of some infirmity, or because of fatigue, is changed into some degree of dimness or into some degree of weakness. So it happens very often, owing to the membrane of the pupil becoming suffused with blood, on account of some corruption produced by weakness, that things all appear of a red colour; and therefore the star appears so coloured. And owing to the sight being weakened, there results in it some dispersion of the spirit, so that things do not appear united, but scattered, almost in the same way as our writing does on a wet piece of paper. And this is the reason why many persons, when they wish to read, remove the paper to some distance from the eyes, in order that the image thereof may come within the eye more easily and more subtly, and thereby the lettering is left impressed on the sight more distinctly and connectedly. For like reason the star also may appear blurred; and I had experience of this in the same year in which this Song was born, for, by trying the eyes very much in the labour of reading, the visual spirits were so weakened that the stars all appeared to me to be blurred by some white mist: and by means of long repose in shady and cool places, and by cooling the ball of the eye with spring water, I re-united the scattered powers, which I restored to their former good condition.

And thus, for the reasons mentioned above, there are many visible causes why the star can appear to us different to what it really is.

CHAPTER X.

LEAVING this digression, which has been needful for seeing the Truth, I return to the proposition, and I say that, as our eyes call, that is, judge, the star other than it really is as to its true condition, so this little ballad judged this Lady according to appearance, other than the Truth, through infirmity of the Soul, which was impassioned with too much desire. And this I make evident when I say that "fear possessed her soul." For this which I saw in her presence appeared fierce or proud to me. Where it is to be known that in proportion as the agent is more closely united to the patient, so much the more powerful is the passion, as may be understood from the opinion of the Philosopher in his book On Generation. Wherefore in proportion as the desired thing draws nigh to the person who desires it, so much the greater is the desire; and the Soul, more impassioned, unites itself more closely to the carnal part, and abandons reason more and more; so that the individual no longer judges like a man, but almost like some other animal, even according to appearance, not discerning the Truth. And this is the reason why the countenance, modest according to the truth, appears disdainful and proud in her.

And that little ballad spoke, according to that judgment, as sensual and irrational at once. And herein it is sufficiently understood that this Song judges this Lady according to Truth, by the disagreement which it has with that other Song of harmony between it and that ballad. And not without reason I say, "When I come near to her glance," and not when she comes within mine. But in this I wish to express the great power which her eyes had over me; for, as if I had been transparent, through every part their light shone through me. And here it would be possible to assign reasons natural and supernatural, but let it suffice here to have said as much as I have; elsewhere I will discourse of it more suitably. Then when I say, "Be such excuse allowed," I impose on the Song instruction how, by the assigned reasons, it may excuse itself there where that is needful, namely, where there may be any suspicion of this opposition; for there is no more to say, except that whoever may feel doubtful as to the matter wherein this Song differs from the other, let him look at the reason which has been here stated. And such a figure as this is quite laudable in Rhetoric, and even necessary when the words are to one person and the intention is to another; because it is always praiseworthy to admonish and necessary also; but it is not always suitable in the mouth of every one. Wherefore, when the son is aware of the vice of the father, and when the subject is aware of the vice of the lord, and when the friend knows that the shame of his friend would be increased to him by admonition from him, when he knows that it would detract from his honour, or when he knows that his friend would not be patient, but enraged at the admonition, this figure is most beautiful and most useful. You may term it dissimulation; it is similar to the work of that wise warrior who attacked the castle on one side in order to draw off the defence from the other, for the attack and the design of the commander are not aimed at one and the same part.

Also, I lay a command on this Song, that it ask permission of this Lady to speak of her; whereby one may infer that a man ought not to be presumptuous in praising another, ought not to take it for granted in his own mind that it is pleasing to the person praised, because often, when some one believes he is bestowing praise, it is taken as blame, either through defect of the speaker or through defect of him who hears. Wherefore it is requisite to have much discretion in this matter; which discretion is tantamount to asking permission, in the way in which I say that this Song or Poem should ask for it.

And thus ends the whole Literal meaning of this treatise; wherefore the order of the work now requires the Allegorical exposition, following the Truth, to be proceeded with.

CHAPTER XI.

Returning now, as the order requires, to the beginning of the Song, I say that this Lady is that Lady of the Intellect who is called Philosophy. But naturally praise excites a desire to know the person praised; and to know the thing may be to know what it is considered to be in itself, and in all that pertains to it, as the Philosopher says in the beginning of the book On Physics; and the name may reveal this when it bears some meaning, as he says in the fourth chapter of the Metaphysics, where it is said that the definition is that reason which the name signifies. Here, therefore, it is necessary, before proceeding farther with her praises, to prove and to say what this is that is called Philosophy, what this name signifies; and when this has been demonstrated, the present Allegory will be more efficaciously discussed. And first of all I will state who first gave this name; then I shall proceed to its signification.

I say, then, that anciently in Italy, almost from the beginning of the foundation of Rome, which was seven hundred and fifty years, a little more or less, before the advent of the Saviour, according as Paul Orosius writes, about the time of Numa Pompilius, second king of the Romans, there lived a most noble Philosopher, who was named Pythagoras. And that he might be living about that time appears from something to which Titus Livius alludes incidentally in the first part of his History. And before him they were called the followers of Science, not Philosophers but Wise Men such as were those Seven most ancient Wise Men, who still live in popular fame. The first of them had the name of Solon, the second Chilon, the third Periander, the fourth Talus, the fifth Cleobulus, the sixth Bias, the seventh Pittacus. Pythagoras, being asked if he were considered to be a Wise Man, rejected this name, and stated himself to be not a Wise Man, but a Lover of Wisdom. And from this circumstance it subsequently arose that any man studious to acquire knowledge, was called a Lover of Wisdom, that is, a Philosopher; for inasmuch as "Philo" in Greek is equivalent to "Love" and "sophia" is equivalent to Wisdom, therefore, "Philo and sophia" mean the same as Love of Wisdom. Wherefore it is possible to see that those two words make that name Philosopher, which is as much as to say Lover of Wisdom. Therefore it may be observed that it is not a term of arrogance, but of humility.

From this sprang naturally the word philosophy, as from the word friend springs naturally the word friendship. Wherefore it is possible to see, considering the signification of the first and second word, that philosophy is no other than friendship to wisdom, or rather to knowledge; wherefore to a certain degree it is possible to call every man a philosopher, according to the natural love which generates a desire for knowledge in each individual.

But since the natural passions are common to all men, we do not specify those passions by some distinctive word, applied to some individual who shares our common nature, as when we say, John is the friend of Martin, we do not mean to signify merely the natural love which all men bear to all men, but we mean the friendship founded upon the natural love which is distinct and peculiar to certain individuals. Thus we do not term any one a philosopher because of the love common to us all. It is the intention or meaning of Aristotle, in the eighth book of the Ethics, that that man may be called a friend whose friendship is not concealed from the person beloved, and to whom also the beloved person is a friend, so that the attachment is mutual; and this must be so either for mutual benefit, or for pleasure, or for credit's sake. And thus, in order that a man may be a philosopher, it must be love to Wisdom which makes one of the sides friendly; it must be study and care which make the other side also friendly, so that familiarity and manifestation of benevolence may spring up between them; because without love and without study one cannot be called a philosopher, but there must be both the one and the other.

And as friendship for the sake of pleasure given or for profit is not true friendship, but accidental, as the Ethics demonstrate, so philosophy for delight or profit is not true philosophy, but accidental. Wherefore one ought not to call him a true philosopher who for some pleasure or other may be a friend of Wisdom in some degree; even as there are many who take delight in repeating songs and in studying the same, and who delight in studying Rhetoric and Music, and who avoid and abandon the other Sciences, which are all members of Wisdom's body. One ought not to call him a true philosopher who is the friend of Wisdom for the sake of profit; such as are the Lawyers, Doctors, and almost all the Religious Men, who do not study for the sake of knowledge, but to acquire money or dignity; and if any one would give them that which they seek to acquire, they would not continue to study. And as amongst the various kinds of friendship, that which is for profit may be called the meanest friendship, so such men as these have less share in the name of Philosopher than any other people.

Wherefore as the friendship conceived through honest affection is true and perfect and perpetual, so is that philosophy true and perfect which is generated by upright desire for knowledge, without regard to aught else, and by the goodness of the friendly soul; which is as much as to say, by right appetite and right reason. And it is possible to say here that as true friendship amongst men is, that each love each entirely, so the true Philosopher loves each part of Wisdom, and Wisdom each part of the Philosopher, so as to draw him wholly to herself, and to allow no thought of his to stray away to other things. Wherefore Wisdom herself says in the Proverbs of Solomon, "I love those who love me." And as true friendship of the mind, considered in itself alone, has for its subject the knowledge of good effects, and for its form the desire for the same, even so Philosophy considered in itself alone, apart from the Soul, has understanding for its subject, and for its form an almost divine love to intellect.

And as the efficient cause of true friendship is Virtue, so the efficient cause of Philosophy is Truth. And as the end of true friendship is true affection, which proceeds from the intercourse proper to Humanity, that is, according to the dictates of Reason, as Aristotle seems to think in the ninth book of the Ethics, so the end of Philosophy is that most excellent affection which suffers no intermission or defect, that is, the true happiness which is acquired by the contemplation of Truth.

And thus it is now possible to see who this my

Lady is, in all her causes and in her whole reason, and why she is called Philosophy; and who is a true Philosopher, and who is one by accident.

But in some fervour or heat of mind the one and the other end of the acts and of the passions are called by the word for the act itself or the passion; as Virgil does in the second book of the Æneid, where he calls Hector, "Oh, light" (which was the act) "and hope" (which is the passion) "of the Trojans:" for he was neither the light nor the hope, but he was the end whence came to them their light in council, and he was the end in which was reposed their hope of safety: as Statius writes in the fifth book of the Thebaid, when Hypsipyle says to Archemorus, "Oh, consolation of things and of the lost country! oh, honour of my servitude!" even as we say daily, showing the friend, "See my friendship;" and the father says to the son, "My love;" and so it is that, through long custom, the Sciences, in which most fervently Philosophy finds the end to which she looks, are called by her name, such as the Natural Science, the Moral Science, and the Metaphysical Science, which last, because most necessarily she looks to her end in that chiefly and most fervently, is called the First Philosophy.

Now, therefore, since it has been seen what the true Philosophy is in its essence; which is that Lady of whom I speak; how her noble name through custom is communicated to the Sciences, and the first science is called the First Philosophy, I may proceed further with her praise.

CHAPTER XII.

IN the first chapter of this treatise the reason which moved me to this Song is so fully discussed that it is no longer necessary to discuss it further, for one can easily enough recall to mind what has been said in this exposition: and therefore, following the divisions made for the Literal meaning, I shall run through the Song, turning back to the sense of the letter where it may be needful. I say, "Love, reasoning of my Lady in my mind." By Love I mean the labour and pains I took to acquire the love of this Lady. If one wishes to know what labour, it can be here considered in two ways. There is one study which leads the man to the daily use of Art and Science; there is another study which he will employ in the acquired use. The first is that which I call Love, which fills my mind continually with new and most exalted ideas of this Lady: even as the anxious pains which one takes to acquire a friendship are wont to do; for, when desiring that friendship, a man is wont to take anxious thought concerning it. This is that study and that affection which usually precedes in men the begetting of the friendship, when already on one side Love is born, and desires and strives that it may be on the other; for, as is said above, Philosophy is born when the Soul and Wisdom have become friends, so that the one is loved by the other.

Neither is it again needful to discuss that first stanza in the present explanation, which was reasoned out as the Proem in the Literal exposition; since, from the first argument thereof, it is easy enough to make out the meaning in this the second one.

We may proceed, then, to the second part, which begins the treatise, and to that place where I say, "The Sun sees not in travel round the Earth." Here it is to be known that as, when discoursing of a sensible thing, one handles it suitably by means of an insensible thing, so of an intelligible thing, one fitly argues by means of an unintelligible. In the Literal sense one speaks of the Sun as a substantial and sensible body; so now it is fit, by image of the Sun, to discourse of the Spiritual and Unintelligible, that is, God.

There is no visible thing in all the world more worthy to serve as a type of God than the Sun, which illuminates with visible light itself first, and then all the celestial and elemental bodies. Thus, God illuminates Himself first with intellectual light, and then the celestial and other intelligible beings. The Sun vivifies all things with his heat, and if anything is destroyed thereby, it is not by the intention of the cause, but it is an accidental effect: thus God vivifies all things in His Goodness, and, if any suffer evil, it is not by the Divine intention, but the effect is accidental. For, if God made the Angels good and evil, He did not make both by intention, but He made the good only; there followed afterwards, beyond His intention, the wickedness of the evil ones; but not so far beyond His intention that God could not foreknow in Himself their wickedness; but so great was the loving desire to produce the Spiritual creature that the foreknowledge that some would come to a bad end neither could nor should prevent God from continuing the production; as it would not be to the praise of Nature if, knowing of herself that the flowers of a tree in a certain part must perish, she should refuse to produce flowers on that tree, and should abandon the production of fruit-bearing trees as vain and useless. I say, then, that God, who encircles and understands all, in His encircling and His understanding sees nothing so gentle, so noble, as He sees when He shines on this Philosophy. For, although God Himself, beholding, may see all things together, inasmuch as the distinction of things is in Him in the same way as the effect is in the cause, yet He sees those things also apart and distinct. He sees, then, this Lady the most noble of all absolutely, inasmuch as most perfectly He sees her in Himself and in her essence. If what has been said above be recalled to mind, Philosophy is a loving use of Wisdom; which especially is in God, because in Him is Supreme Wisdom, and Supreme Love, and Supreme Action; which cannot be elsewhere except inasmuch as it proceeds from Him. It is, then, the Divine Philosophy of the Divine Being, since in Him nothing can be that is not part of His Essence; and it is most noble, because the Divine Essence is most noble, and it is in Him in a manner perfect and true, as if by eternal wedlock; it is in the other Intelligences in a less degree, as if platonic, as if a virgin love from whom no lover receives full and complete joy, but contents himself by gazing on the beauty of her countenance. Wherefore it is possible to say that God sees not, that He does not intently regard, anything so noble as this Lady; I say anything, inasmuch as He sees and distinguishes the other things, as has been said, seeing Himself to be the cause of all. Oh, most noble and most excellent heart, which is at peace in the bride of the Ruler of Heaven; and not bride only, but sister, and the daughter beloved above all others.

CHAPTER XIII.

HAVING seen in the beginning of the praises of this Lady how subtly it is said that she is of the Divine Substance, as was first to be considered, we proceed now to consider her as she is in the Intelligences that proceed thence. "All minds of Heaven wonder at her worth," where it is to be known that I say, "minds of Heaven," making that allusion to God which has been mentioned above; and from this one excludes the Intelligences who are exiled from the eternal country, who can never study Philosophy, because love in them is entirely extinct, and for the study of Philosophy, as has been already said, Love is necessary. One sees, therefore, that the spirits of Hell are deprived of the sight of this most beautiful Lady; and, since she is the blessing of the intellect, the deprivation of her is most bitter and full of every sadness.

Then, when I say, "Mortals, enamoured, find her in their thought," I descend to show how she also may come into the Human Intelligence in a secondary degree; with which Human Philosophy I then proceed through the treatise, praising it. I say, then, that the mortals who "find her in their thought" in this life do not always find her there, but only "When Love his peace into their hearts has brought;" wherein there are to be seen three points which are alluded to in this text.

The first is when one says, "Mortals, enamoured,"

because it seems to make a distinction in the human race, and of necessity it must be made; for, according to what manifestly appears, and which in the following treatise will be specially reasoned out, the greatest part of men live more according to the Sense than according to Reason; and those who live according to the Sense can never be enamoured of this Lady, since of her they can have no apprehension whatever.

The second point is when it says, "When Love his peace into their minds has brought," where it appears to make a distinction of time. And that is necessary; for, although the separate Intelligences gaze at this Lady continually, the Human Intelligence cannot do so; since Human Nature, besides that which gives delight to the Intellect and the Reason, has need of many things requisite for its support which contemplation cannot furnish forth. Therefore our Wisdom is sometimes habitual only, and not actual; and this does not happen to the other Intelligences, which alone are perfect in their intellectual nature. And so, when our soul is not in the act of contemplation, one cannot truly say that it is in Philosophy, except inasmuch as it has the habit of it, and the power of being able to arouse it; sometimes, therefore, she is with the people who are enamoured of her here below, and sometimes not.

The third point is, when it speaks of the time when those people are with her, namely, when Love has brought into their minds his peace; which means no other than when the man is in the act of contemplation, since he does not strive to feel the peace of that Lady except in the act of contemplation.

And thus one sees how this Lady is firstly in the Mind of God, secondly in the other separate Intelligences through continual contemplation, and afterwards in the human intellect through interpreted contemplation. But the man who has her for his Lady is ever to be termed a Philosopher, notwithstanding that he may not be always in the final act of Philosophy, for it is usual to name other men after their habits. Wherefore we call any man virtuous, not merely when performing virtuous actions, but from having the habit or custom of virtue. And we call a man eloquent, even when he is not speaking, from his habit of eloquence, that is, of speaking well.

And of this Philosophy, in which Human Intelligence has part, there will now be the following encomiums to prove how great a part of her good gifts is bestowed on Human Nature. I say, then, afterwards:

> Her Maker saw that she was good, and poured,
>   Beyond our Nature, fulness of His Power
>   On her pure Soul, whence shone this holy dower
> Through all her frame.

For the capacity of our Nature is subdued by it, which it makes beautiful and virtuous. Wherefore, although into the habit of that Lady one may somewhat come, it is not possible to say that any one who enters thereinto properly has that habit; since the first study, that whereby the habit is begotten, cannot perfectly acquire that philosophy. And here one sees her lowly praise; for, perfect or imperfect, she never loses the name of perfection. And because of this her surpassing excellence, it says that the Soul of Philosophy "shone Through all her frame," that is, that God ever imparts to her of His Light.

Here we may recall to mind what is said above,

that Love is a form of Philosophy, and therefore here is called her Soul ; which Love is manifest in the use of Wisdom, and such use brings with it a wonderful beauty, that is to say, contentment under any condition of the time, and contempt for those things which other men make their masters.

Wherefore it happens that those other unhappy ones who gaze thereon, and think over their own defects from the desire for perfection, fall into the weariness of sighs ; and this is meant where it says : " That from the eyes she touches heralds fly Heartward with longings, heavenward with a sigh."

CHAPTER XIV.

As in the Literal exposition, after the general praises one descends to the especial, firstly on the part of the Soul, then on the part of the body, so now the text proceeds after the general encomium to descend to the especial commendation. As it is said above, Philosophy here has Wisdom for its material subject and Love for its form, and the habit of contemplation for the union of the two. Wherefore in this passage which subsequently begins, " On her fair form Virtue Divine descends," I mean to praise Love, which is part of Philosophy. Here it is to be known that for a virtue to descend from one thing into another there is no other way than to reduce that thing into its own similitude ; as we see evidently in the natural agents, for their virtue descending into the things that are the patients, they bring those things into their similitude as far as they are able to attain it.

We see that the Sun, pouring his rays down on this Earth, reduces the things thereon to his own similitude of light in proportion as they by their own disposition are able to receive light of his light. Thus, I say that God reduces this Love to His own Similitude as much as it is possible for it to bear likeness to Him. And it alludes to the nature of the creative act, saying, "As on the Angel that beholds His face." Where again it is to be known that the first Agent, who is God, paints His Virtue on some things by means of direct radiance, and on some things by means of reflected splendour; wherefore into the separate Intelligences the Divine Light shines without any interposing medium; into the others it is reflected from those Intelligences which were first illumined.

But since mention is here made of Light and Splendour, for the more perfect understanding thereof I will show the difference between those words, according to the opinion of Avicenna. I say that it is the custom of Philosophers to speak of Heaven as Light, inasmuch as Light is there in its primeval Spring, or its first origin. They speak of it as a ray of Light while it passes through the medium from its source into the first body in which it has its end; they call it Splendour where it is reflected back from some part that has received illumination. I say, then, that the Divine Virtue or Power draws this Love into Its Own Similitude without any interposing medium.

And it is possible to make this evident, especially in this, that as the Divine Love is Eternal, so must its object of necessity be eternal, so that those things are eternal which He loves. And thus it makes this Love to love, for the Wisdom into which this Love strikes is eternal. Wherefore it is written of her: "From the beginning, before Time was created, I am: and in the Time to come I shall not fail." And in the Proverbs of Solomon this Wisdom says: "I am established for ever." And in the beginning of the Gospel of John, her eternity is openly alluded to, as it is possible to observe. And therefore it results that there, where this Love shines, all the other Loves become obscure and almost extinct, since its eternal object subdues and overpowers all other objects in a manner beyond all comparison; and therefore the most excellent Philosophers in their actions openly demonstrate it, whereby we know that they have treated all other things with indifference except Wisdom. Wherefore Democritus, neglecting all care of his own person, trimmed neither his beard, nor the hair of his head, nor his nails. Plato, indifferent to the riches of this world, despised the royal dignity, for he was the son of a king. Aristotle, caring for no other friend, combated with his own best friend, even with the above-named Plato, his dearest friend after Philosophy. And why do we speak of these, when we find others who, for these thoughts, held their life in contempt, such as Zeno, Socrates, Seneca, and many more? It is evident, therefore, that in this Love the Divine Power, after the manner of an Angel, descends into men; and to give proof of this, the text presently exclaims: "Fair one who doubt, go with her, mark the grace In all her acts." By "Fair one" is meant the noble soul of judgment, free in its own power, which is Reason; hence the other souls cannot be called Ladies, but handmaids, since they are not for themselves, but for others; and the Philosopher says, in the first book of Metaphysics, that

that thing is free which is a cause of itself and not for others. It says, "go with her, mark the grace In all her acts," that is, make thyself the companion of this Love, and look at that which will be found within it; and in part it alludes to this, saying, "Downward from Heaven bends An Angel when she speaks," meaning that where Philosophy is in action a celestial thought stoops down, in which this being reasons or discourses beyond the power of Human Nature.

The Song says "from Heaven," to give people to understand that not only Philosophy, but the thoughts friendly to it, are abstracted from all low and earthly things. Then afterwards it says how she strengthens and kindles love wherever she appears with the sweet persuasions of her actions, which are in all her aspects modest, gentle, and without any domineering assumption. And subsequently, by still greater persuasion to induce a desire for her company, it says: "Fair in all like her, fairest she'll appear Who is most like her." Again it adds: "We, content to call Her face a Miracle," find help in it, where it is to be known that the regard of this Lady was freely ordained to arouse a desire in us for its acquisition, not only in her countenance, which she reveals to sight, but also in the things which she keeps hidden. Wherefore as, through her, much of that which is hidden is seen by means of Reason (and consequently to see by Reason without her seems a miracle), so, through her, one believes each miracle in the action of a higher intellectual Power to have reason, and therefore to be possible. From whence true Faith has its origin, from which comes the Hope to desire the Future, and from that are born the works of Charity, by which three Virtues we mount to become Philosophers in that celestial Athens where Stoics, Peripatetics, and Epicureans, by the practice of Eternal Truth, concur harmoniously in one desire.

CHAPTER XV.

IN the preceding chapter this glorious Lady is praised according to one of her component parts, that is, Love. In this chapter I intend to explain that passage which begins, "Her aspect shows delights of Paradise," and here it is requisite to discuss and praise her other part, Wisdom.

The text then says that in the face of this Lady things appear which show us joys of Paradise; and it distinguishes the place where this appears, namely, in the eyes and the smile. And here it must be known that the eyes of Wisdom are her demonstrations, whereby one sees the Truth most certainly; but her persuasions are in her smile, in which persuasions the inner Light of Wisdom reveals itself without any veil or concealment. And in these two is felt that most exalted joy which is the supreme good in Paradise. This joy cannot be in any other thing here below, except in gazing into these eyes and upon that smile. And the reason is this, that since each thing naturally desires its perfection, without which it cannot be at peace, to have that is to be blessed. For although it might possess all other things, yet, being without that, there would remain in it desire, which cannot consist with perfect happiness, since perfect happiness is a perfect thing, and desire is a defective thing. For one desires not that which he has, but that which he has not, and here is a manifest defect. And in this form solely can human perfection be acquired, as the perfection of Reason, on which, as on its principal part, our essential being all depends. All our other actions, as to feel or hear, to take food, and the rest, are through this one alone; and this is for itself, and not for others. So that, if that be perfect, it is so perfect that the man, inasmuch as he is a man, sees each desire fulfilled, and thus he is happy. And therefore it is said in the Book of Wisdom: "Whoso casteth away Wisdom and Knowledge is unhappy," that is to say, he suffers the privation of happiness. From the habit of Wisdom it follows that a man learns to be happy and content, according to the opinion of the Philosopher. One sees, then, how in the aspect of this Lady joys of Paradise appear, and therefore one reads in the Book of Wisdom quoted above, when speaking of her, "She is a shining whiteness of the Eternal Light; a Mirror without blemish, of the Majesty of God." Then when it says, "Things over which the intellect may stray," I excuse myself, saying that I can say but little concerning these, on account of their overpowering influence. Where it is to be known that in any way these things dazzle our intellect, inasmuch as they affirm certain things to be, which our intellect is unable to comprehend, that is, God and Eternity, and the first Matter which most certainly they do not see, and with all faith they believe to be. And even what they are we cannot understand; and so, by not denying things, it is possible to draw near to some knowledge of them, but not otherwise.

Truly here it is possible to have some very strong doubt how it is that Wisdom can make the man completely happy without being able to show him certain things perfectly; since the natural desire for knowledge is in the man, and without fulfilment of the desire he cannot be fully happy. To this it is possible to reply clearly, that the natural desire in each thing is in proportion to the possibility of reaching to the thing desired; otherwise it would pass into opposition to itself, which is impossible; and Nature would have worked in vain, which also is impossible.

It would pass into opposition, for, desiring its perfection, it would desire its imperfection, since he would desire always to desire, and never fulfil his desire. And into this error the cursed miser falls, and does not perceive that he desires always to desire, going backwards to reach to an impossible amount.

Nature also would have worked in vain, since it would not be ordained to any end; and, in fact, human desire is proportioned in this life to that knowledge which it is possible to have here. One cannot pass that point except through error, which is outside the natural intention. And thus it is proportioned in the Angelic, and it is limited in Human Nature, and it finds its end in that Wisdom in proportion as the nature of each can apprehend it.

And this is the reason why the Saints have no envy amongst themselves, since each one attains the end of his desire, and the desire of each is in due proportion to the nature of his goodness. Wherefore, since to know God and certain other things, as Eternity and the first Matter, is not possible to our Nature, naturally we have no desire for that knowledge, and hereby is this doubtful question solved.

Then when I say, "Rain from her beauty little

flames of fire," I proceed to another joy of Paradise, that is, from the secondary felicity, happiness, to this first one, which proceeds from her beauty, where it is to be known that <u>Morality is the beauty of Philosophy.</u> For as the beauty of the body is the result of its members in proportion as they are fitly ordered, so the beauty of Wisdom, which is the body of Philosophy, as has been said, results from the order of the Moral Virtues which visibly make that joy. And therefore I say that her beauty, which is Morality, rains down little flames of fire, meaning direct desire, which is begotten in the pleasure of the Moral Doctrine; which desire removes it again from the natural vices, and not only from the others. And thence springs that happiness which Aristotle defined in the first book of Ethics, saying, that it is Work according to Virtue in the Perfect Life.

And when it says, "Fair one, who may desire Escape from blame," it proceeds in praise of Philosophy. I cry aloud to the people that they should follow her, telling them of her good gifts, that is to say, that by following her each one may become good Therefore it says to each Soul, that feels its beauty is to blame because it does not appear what it ought to appear, let her look at this example. Where it is to be known that the Morals are the beauty of the Soul, that is to say, the most excellent virtues, which sometimes through vanity or through pride are made less beautiful or less agreeable, as in the last treatise it was possible to perceive. And therefore I say that, in order to shun this, one looks at that Lady, Philosophy, there where she is the example of Humility, namely, in that part of herself which is called Moral Philosophy. And I subjoin that by gazing at her (I say, at Wisdom) in that part, every vicious man will become upright and good. And therefore I say she has "a spirit to create Good thoughts, and crush the vices." She turns gently back him who has gone astray from the right course.

Finally, in highest praise of Wisdom, I say of her that she is the Mother of every good Principle, saying that she is "God's thought," who began the World, and especially the movement of the Heaven by which all things are generated, and wherein each movement has its origin, that is to say, that the Divine Thought is Wisdom. She was, when God made the World; whence it follows that she could make it, and therefore Solomon said in the Book of Proverbs, in the person of Wisdom: "When He prepared the Heavens, I was there: when He set a compass upon the face of the depth; when He established the clouds above; when He strengthened the fountains of the deep; when He gave to the sea His decree, that the waters should not pass His commandment; when He appointed the foundations of the Earth: then I was by Him, as one brought up with Him, and I was daily His delight, rejoicing always before Him." O, ye Men, worse than dead, who fly from the friendship of Wisdom, open your eyes, and see that before you were she was the Lover of you, preparing and ordaining the process of your being! Since you were made she came that she might guide you, came to you in your own likeness; and, if all of you cannot come into her presence, honour her in her friends, and follow their counsels, as of them who announce to you the will of this eternal Empress! Close not your ears to Solomon, who tells you "the path of the Just is as a shining Light, which goeth forth and increaseth even to the day of salvation." Follow after them, behold their works, which ought to be to you as a beacon of light for guidance in the path of this most brief life.

And here we may close the Commentary on the true meaning of the present Song. The last stanza, which is intended for a refrain, can be explained easily enough by the Literal exposition, except inasmuch as it says that I there called this Lady "disdainful and morose." Where it is to be known that at the beginning this Philosophy appeared to me on the part of her body, which is Wisdom, morose, for she smiled not on me, insomuch that as yet I did not understand her persuasions; and she seemed to me disdainful, for she turned not her glance to me, that is to say, I could not see her demonstrations. But the defect was altogether on my side. From this, and from that which is given in the explanation of the Literal meaning of the Song, the Allegory of the refrain is evident. It is time, therefore, that we proceed farther, and this treatise end.

Are temperate in Youth,
  And resolutely strong,
Love much, win praise for courtesy,
  Are loyal, hating wrong.

Are prudent in their Age,
  And generous and just,
And glad at heart to hear and speak
  When good to man's discussed.

The fourth part of their life
  Weds them again to God,
They wait, and contemplate the end,
  And bless the paths they trod.

How many are deceived! My Song,
  Against the strayers : when you reach
Our Lady, hide not from her that your end
  Is labour that would lessen wrong,
  And tell her too, in trusty speech,
I travel ever talking of your Friend.

CHAPTER I.

LOVE, according to the unanimous opinion of the wise men who discourse of him, and as by experience we see continually, is that which brings together and unites the lover with the beloved ; wherefore Pythagoras says, "In friendship many become one."

And the things which are united naturally communicate their qualities to each other, insomuch that sometimes it happens that one is wholly changed into the nature of the other, the result being that the passions of the beloved person enter into the person of the lover, so that the love of the one is communicated to the other, and so likewise hatred, desire, and every other passion ; wherefore the friends of the one are beloved by the other, and the enemies hated; and so in the Greek proverb it is said: "With friends all things ought to be in common."

Wherefore I, having made a friend of this Lady, mentioned above in the truthful exposition, began to love and to hate according to her love and her hatred. I then began to love the followers of Truth, and to hate the followers of Error and Falsehood, even as she does. But since each thing is to be loved for itself and none are to be hated except for excess of evil, it is reasonable and upright to hate not the things, but the evil in the things, and to endeavour to distinguish between these. And if any person has this intention, my most excellent Lady understands especially how to distinguish the evil in anything, which is the cause of hate; since in her is all Reason, and in her is the fountain-head of all uprightness.

I, following her as much as I could in her work as in her love, abominated and despised the errors of the people with infamy or reproach, not cast on those lost in error, but on the errors themselves; by blaming which, I thought to create displeasure and to separate the displeased ones from those faults in them which were hated by me. Amongst which errors one especially I reproved, which, because it is hurtful and dangerous not only to those who remain in it, but also to others who reprove it, I separate it from them and condemn.

This is the error concerning Human Goodness, which, inasmuch as it is sown in us by Nature, ought to be termed Nobility; which error was so strongly entrenched by evil custom and by weak intellect that the opinion of almost all people was falsified or deceived by it; and from the false opinion sprang false judgments, and from false judgments sprang unjust reverence and unjust contempt; wherefore the good were held in vile disdain, and the evil were honoured and exalted. This was the worst confusion in the world; even as he can see who looks subtly at that which may result from it. And though it seemed that this my Lady had somewhat changed her sweet countenance towards me, especially where I gazed and sought to discover whether the first Matter of the Elements was created by God, for which reason I strengthened myself to frequent her presence a little, as if remaining there with her assent, I began to consider in my mind the fault of man concerning the said error. And to shun sloth, which is an especial enemy of this Lady, and to describe or state this error very clearly, this error which robs her of so many friends, I proposed to cry aloud to the people who are walking in the path of evil, in order that they might direct their steps to the right road; and I began a Song, in the beginning of which I said, "Soft rhymes of love I used to find,' wherein I intend to lead the people back into the right path, the path of right knowledge concerning true Nobility, as by the knowledge of its text, to the explanation of which I now turn my attention, any one will be able to perceive.

And since the intention of this Song is directed to a remedy so requisite, it was not well to speak under any figure of speech; but it was needful to prepare this medicine speedily, that speedy might be the restoration to health, which, being so corrupted, hastened to a hideous death. It will not, then, be requisite in the exposition of this Song to unveil any allegory, but simply to discuss its meaning according to the letter. By my Lady I always mean her who is spoken of in the preceding Song, that is to say, that Light of supreme virtue, Philosophy, whose rays cause the flowers of true Nobility to blossom forth in mankind and to bear fruit in the sons of men ; concerning which true Nobility the proposed Song fully intends to treat.

CHAPTER II.

IN the beginning of the explanation now undertaken, in order to render the meaning of the proposed Song more clear and distinct, it is requisite to divide that first part into two parts, for in the first part one speaks in the manner of a Proem or Preface ; in the second, the subject under discussion is continued ; and the second part begins in the commencement of the stanza, where it says :

> One raised to Empire held,
> As far as he could see,
> Descent of wealth, and generous ways,
> To make Nobility.

The first part, again, can be comprehended in three divisions or members. In the first it states why I depart from my usual mode of speech ; in the second, I say of what it is my intention to discourse ; in the third, I call upon that Helper who most can aid me to establish Truth. The second member, clause, or division begins : "And since time suits me now." The third begins : " First calling on that Lord." I say then that I was compelled to abandon the soft rhymes of Love which I was accustomed to search for in my thoughts, and I assign the reason or cause ; wherefore I say that it is not because I have given up all intention of making rhymes of Love, but because new aspects have appeared in my Lady which have deprived me of material for present speech of Love. Where it is to be known that it does not here say that the gestures of this Lady are disdainful and angry according to appearance only, as may be seen in the tenth chapter of the preceding treatise; for at another time I say that the appearance is contrary to the Truth; and how this can be, how one self-same thing can be sweet and appear bitter, or rather be clear and appear obscure, may there be seen clearly enough.

Afterwards when I say, "And since time suits," I say, even as has been said, what that is whereof I intend to discourse. And that which it says in the words "time suits" is not here to be passed over with a dry foot, because there is a most powerful reason for my action; but it is to be seen how reasonably time must wait on all our acts, and especially on speech.

Time, according to what Aristotle says in the fourth chapter of Physics, is the number of movement, first, second, and onwards; and the number of the celestial movement, which prepares the things here below to receive in various ways any informing power. For the Earth is prepared in one way in the beginning of Spring to receive into itself the informing power of the herbs and flowers, and the Winter otherwise; and in one manner is one season prepared to receive the seed, differing from another. And even so our Mind, inasmuch as it is founded upon the temper of the body, which has to follow the revolution of the Heaven, at one time is disposed in one way, at another time in another way; wherefore words, which are, as it were, the seeds of actions, ought very discreetly to be withheld or uttered; they should be spoken with such sound judgment that they may be well received, and good fruit follow from them; not withheld or spent so sparingly that barrenness is the result of their defective utterance. And therefore a suitable time should be chosen, both for him who speaks and for him who must hear: for if the speaker is badly prepared, very often his words are injurious or hurtful; and if the hearer is ill-disposed, those words which are good are ill received. And therefore Solomon says in Ecclesiastes: "There is a time to speak, and a time to be silent." Wherefore I, feeling within myself that my disposition to speak of Love was disturbed, for the cause which has been mentioned in the preceding chapter, it seemed to me that the time might suit me now, time which bears with it the fulfilment of every desire, and appears in the guise of a generous giver to those who grudge not to await him patiently. Wherefore St. James says in his Epistle, in the fifth chapter: "Behold, the husbandman waiteth for the precious fruit of the Earth, and hath long patience for it, until he receive the early and the latter rain." For all our sorrows, or cares, or vexations, if we inquire diligently into their origin, proceed, as it were, from not knowing the use of time. I say, "since the time suits," I will leave my pen alone, that is to say, the sweet or gentle style I used when I sang of Love; and I say that I will speak of that worth whereby a man is truly noble.

And as it is possible to understand worth in many ways, here I intend to assume worth to be a power of Nature, or rather a goodness bestowed by her, as will be seen in what follows; and I promise to discourse on this subject with a "rhyme subtle and severe."

Wherefore it is requisite to know that rhyme may be considered in a double sense, that is to say, in a wide and in a narrow sense. In the narrow sense, it is understood as that concordance which in the last and in the penultimate syllable it is usual to make. In the wide sense, it is understood for all that language which, with numbers and regulated time, falls into rhymed consonance; and thus it is desired that it should be taken and understood in this Proem. And therefore it says "severe," with reference to the sound of the style, which to such a subject must not be sweet and pleasing; and it says "subtle," with regard to the meaning of the words, which proceed with subtle argument and disputation.

And I subjoin: "hold false and vile The judgment;" where again it is promised to confute the judgment of the people full of error: false, that is, removed from the Truth; and vile, that is to say, affirmed and fortified by vileness of mind. And it is to be observed that in this Proem I promise, firstly, to treat of the Truth, and then to confute the False; and in the treatise the opposite is done, for, in the first place, I confute the False, and then treat of the Truth, which does not appear rightly according to the promise. And therefore it is to be known that, although the intention is to speak of both, the principal intention is to handle the Truth; and the intention is to reprove the False or Untrue, in so far as by so doing I make the Truth appear more excellent.

And here, in the first place, the promise is to speak of the Truth according to the chief intention, which creates in the minds of the hearers a desire to hear; for in the first treatise I reprove the False or

Untrue in order that, the false opinions being chased away, the Truth may be received more freely. And this method was adopted by the master of human argument, Aristotle, who always in the first place fought with the adversaries of Truth, and then, having vanquished them, revealed or demonstrated Truth itself.

Finally, when I say, "First calling on that Lord," I appeal to Truth to be with me, Truth being that Lord who dwells in the eyes of Philosophy, that is to say, in her demonstrations. And indeed Truth is that Lord; for the Soul espoused to Truth is the bride of Truth, and otherwise it is a slave or servant deprived of all liberty.

And it says, "my Lady learnt Herself to love and prize," because this Philosophy, which has been said in the preceding treatise to be a loving use of Wisdom, beholds herself when the beauty of her eyes appears to her. And what else is there to be said, except that the Philosophic Soul not only contemplates this Truth, but again contemplates her own contemplation and the beauty of that, again revolving upon herself, and being enamoured with herself on account of the beauty of her first glance?

And thus ends this which, as a Proem or Preface in three divisions, heads the present treatise.

CHAPTER III.

HAVING seen the meaning of the Proem, we must now follow the treatise, and, to demonstrate it clearly, it must be divided into its chief parts, which are three.

In the first, one treats of Nobility according to the opinion of other men; in the second, one treats of it according to the true opinion; in the third, one addresses speech to the Song by way of ornament to that which has been said. The second part begins: "I say that from one root Each Virtue firstly springs." The third begins: "How many are deceived! My Song, Against the strayers." And after these general parts, it will be right to make other divisions, in order to make the meaning of the demonstration clear. Therefore, let no one marvel if it proceed with many divisions, since a great and high work is now on my hands, and one that is but little entered upon by authors; the treatise must be long and subtle into which the reader now enters with me, if I am to unfold perfectly the text according to the meaning which it bears.

I say, then, that this first part is now divided into two: for in the first, the opinions of others are placed; in the second, those opinions are confuted; and this second part begins: "Whoever shall define The man a living tree." Again, the first part which remains has two clauses: the first is the variation of the opinion of the Emperor; the second is the variation of the opinion of the Common People, which is naked or void of all reason; and this second clause or division begins: "Another, lightly wise." I say then, "One raised to Empire," that is to say, such an one made use of the Imperial Office. Where it is to be known that Frederick of Suabia, the last Emperor of the Romans (I say last with respect to the present time, notwithstanding that Rudolf, and Adolphus, and Albert were elected after his death and from his descendants), being asked what Nobility might be, replied that "it was ancient wealth, and good manners."

And I say that there was another of less wisdom, who, pondering and revolving this definition in every part, removed the last particle, that is, the good manners, and held to the first, that is, to the ancient riches. And as he seems to have doubted the text, perhaps through not having good manners, and not wishing to lose the title of Nobility, he defined it according to that which made himself noble, namely, possession of ancient wealth.

And I say that this opinion is that of almost all, saying that after it go all the people who make those men noble who have a long pedigree, and who have been rich through many generations; since in this cry do almost all men bark.

These two opinions (although one, as has been said, is of no consequence whatever) seem to have two very grave arguments in support of them. The first is, that the Philosopher says that whatever appears true to the greatest number cannot be entirely false. The second is, the authority of the definition by an Emperor. And that one may the better see the power of the Truth, which conquers all other authority, I intend to argue with the one reason as with the other, to which it is a strong helper and powerful aid.

And, firstly, one cannot understand Imperial authority until the roots of it are found. It is our intention to treat or discourse of them in an especial chapter.

CHAPTER IV.

THE radical foundation of Imperial Majesty, according to the Truth, is the necessity of Human Civilization, which is ordained to one end, that is, to a Happy Life. Nothing is of itself sufficient to attain this without some external help, since man has need of many things which one person alone is unable to obtain. And therefore the Philosopher says that man is naturally a companionable animal. And as a man requires for his sufficient comfort the domestic companionship of a family, so a house requires for its sufficient comfort a neighbourhood; otherwise there would be many wants to endure which would be an obstacle to happiness. And since a neighbourhood cannot satisfy all requirements, there must for the satisfaction of men be the City. Again, the City requires for its Arts and Manufactures to have an environment, as also for its defence, and to have brotherly intercourse with the circumjacent or adjacent Cities, and thence the Kingdom.

But since the human mind in restricted possession of the Earth finds no peace, but always desires to acquire Glory, as we see by experience, discords and wars must arise between realm and realm. These are the tribulation of Cities; and through the Cities, of the neighbourhoods; and through the neighbourhoods, of the houses; and through the houses, of men; and thus is the happiness of man prevented or obstructed. Wherefore, in order to prevent these wars, and to remove the causes of them through all the Earth, so far as it is given to the Human Race to possess it, there must of necessity be Monarchy, that is to say, one sole principality; and there must be one Prince, who, possessing all, and not being able to desire more, holds the Kings content within the limits of the kingdoms, so that peace may be between them, wherein the Cities may repose, and in this rest the neighbouring hamlets may dwell together in mutual love ; in this love the houses obtain all they need, which, being obtained, men can live happily, which is that end for which man was born. And to these reasons might be applied the words of the Philosopher, for he says, in the book On Politics, that when many things are ordained to one end, one of those must be the ruling power, and all the others must be governed by that. Even as we see in a ship that the different offices and the different means to different ends in that ship are ordained to one end alone, that is to say, to reach the desired port by a safe voyage, where as each officer orders his own work to the proper end, even so there is one who considers all these ends, and ordains those to the final one ; and this is the Pilot, whose voice all must obey.

We see this also in the religious bodies and in the military bodies, in all those things which are ordained to one end, as has been said. Wherefore it can plainly be seen that to attain the perfection of the Universal Union of the Human Race there must be one Pilot, as it were, who, considering the different conditions of the World, and ordaining the different and needful offices, may hold or possess over the whole the universal and incontestable office of Command. And this office is well designated Empire, without any addition, because it is of all other governments the government ; and so he who is appointed to this office is designated Emperor, because of all Governors he is the Governor, and what he says is Law to all, and ought by all to be obeyed; and every other government derives vigour and authority from the government of this man. And thus it is evident that the Imperial Majesty and Authority is the most exalted in the Human Family.

No doubt it would be possible for some one to cavil, saying, that although the office of Empire may be required in the World, that does not make the authority of the Roman Prince rationally supreme, which it is the intention of the treatise to prove; since the Roman Power was acquired, not by Reason nor by decree of Universal Election, but by Force, which seems to be opposed to Reason. To this one can easily reply, that the election of this Supreme Official must primarily proceed from that Council which foresees all things, that is, God; otherwise the election would not have been of equal benefit for all the people, since, before the pre-ordained Official, there was none who had the good of all at heart.

And since a gentler nature in ruling, and a stronger in maintaining, and a more subtle in acquiring never was and never will be than that of the Latin People, as one can see by experience, and especially that of the Holy People, in whom was blended the noble Trojan blood; to that office it was elected by God. Wherefore, since, to obtain it, not without very great power could it be approached, and to employ it a most exalted and most humane benignity was required, this was the people which was most fitly prepared for it. Hence not by Force was it assumed in the first place by the Roman People but by Divine Ordinance, which is above all Reason. And Virgil is in harmony with this in the first book of the Æneid, when he says, speaking in the person of God: " On these [that is, on the Romans] I impose no limits to their possessions, nor to their duration; to them I have given boundless Empire." Force, then, was not the moving cause, as he believed who was cavilling; but there was an instrumental cause even as the blows of the hammer are the cause of the knife, and the soul of the workman is the moving and the efficient cause; and thus, not force, but a cause, even a Divine Cause, has been the origin of the Roman Empire.

And that this is so it is possible to see by two most evident reasons, which prove that City to be the Empress, and to have from God an especial birth, and to have from God an especial success. But since in this chapter without too great length it would not be possible to discuss this subject, and long chapters are the enemies of Memory, I will again make a digression in another chapter in order to prove the reasons here alluded to, which are not without utility, and may give great pleasure.

CHAPTER V.

IT is no cause for wonder if the Divine Providence, which surpasses beyond measure all angelic and human foresight, often appears to us to proceed mysteriously, since many times human actions conceal their motives from men. But there is great cause for wonder when the execution of the Eternal Counsel proceeds so evidently that our reason can discern it. And therefore in the beginning of this chapter I can speak with the mouth of Solomon, who, in the person of Wisdom, says in his Proverbs: "Hear, for I will speak of excellent things!"

The Divine Goodness unmeasureable, desiring to conform again to Itself the Human Creature, which, through the sin of the prevarication of the first Man, was separated from God and deformed thereby, it was decided, in that most exalted and most united Divine Consistory of the Trinity, that the Son of God should descend to the Earth to accomplish this union. And since at His advent into the world, not only Heaven, but Earth, must be in the best disposition; and the best disposition of the Earth is when it is a Monarchy, that is to say, all subject to one Prince, as has been said above, by Divine Providence it was ordained what people and what city should fulfil this, and that people was the Roman nation, and that city was glorious Rome. And since the Inn also wherein the Heavenly King must enter must of necessity be most cleanly and most pure, there was ordained a most Holy Race, from which, after many excellent or just ancestors, there should be born a Woman more perfect than all others, who should be the abode of the Son of God. And this race was the Race of David, from which was born the glory and honour of the Human Race, that is to say, Mary. And therefore it is written in Isaiah: "A virgin shall be born of the stem of Jesse, and a branch shall grow out of his roots." And Jesse was the father of the aforesaid David. And it happened at one period of time that when David was born, Rome was born, that is to say, Æneas then came from Troy to Italy, which was the origin of the most noble Roman City, even as the written word bears witness. Evident enough, therefore, is the Divine election of the Roman Empire by the birth of the Holy City, which was contemporaneous with the root of the race from which Mary sprang.

And incidentally it is to be mentioned that, since this Heaven began to revolve, it never was in a better disposition than when He descended from on high, He who had made it and who is its Ruler, even as again by virtue of their arts the Mathematicians may be able to discover. The World never was nor ever will be so perfectly prepared as then, when it was governed by the voice of one man alone, Prince and Commander of the Roman people, even as Luke the Evangelist bears witness. And therefore there was Universal Peace, which never was again nor ever will be, for the Ship of the Human Family rightly by a sweet pathway was hastening to its rightful haven. Oh, ineffable and incomprehensible Wisdom of God, which in Heaven above didst prepare, so long beforehand, for Thy advent into Syria and here in Italy at the same time! And oh, most foolish and vile beasts who pasture in the guise of men—you who presume to speak against our Faith, and profess to know, as ye spin and dig, what God has ordained with so much forethought—curses be on you and your presumption, and on him who believes in you!

And, as has been said above, at the end of the preceding chapter, the Roman People had from God not only an especial birth, but an especial success; for, briefly, from Romulus, who was the first father of Rome, even to its most perfect era, that is, to the time of its predicted Emperor, its success was achieved not only by human, but by Divine means. For if we consider the Seven Kings who first governed it—Romulus, Numa, Tullus, Ancus Martius, Servius Tullius, and the Tarquins, who were, as it were, the nurses and tutors of its Childhood—we shall be able to find, by the written word of Roman History, especially by Titus Livius, those to have been of different natures, according to the opportunity of the advancing tract of time. If we consider, then, its Adolescence, when it was emancipated from the regal tutorship by Brutus, the first Consul, even to Cæsar, its first supreme Prince, we shall find it exalted, not with human, but with Divine citizens, into whom, not human, but Divine love was inspired in loving Rome; and this neither could be nor ought to be, except for an especial end intended by God through such infusion of a heavenly spirit. And who will say that there was no Divine inspiration in Fabricius when he rejected an almost infinite amount of gold because he was unwilling to abandon his country? or in Curius, whom the Samnites attempted to corrupt, who said, when refusing a very large quantity of gold for love of his country, that the Roman citizens did not desire to possess gold, but the possessors of the gold? Who will say there was no Divine inspiration in Mutius burning his own hand because it had failed in the blow wherewith he had thought to deliver Rome? Who will say of Torquatus, who sentenced his own son to death from love to the Public Good, that he could have endured this without a Divine Helper? Who will say this of the Brutus before mentioned? Who will say it of the Decii and of the Drusi, who laid down their lives for their country? Who will say of the captive Regulus of Carthage, sent to Rome to exchange the Carthaginian prisoners for Roman prisoners of war, who, after having explained the object of his embassy, gave counsel against himself, through pure love to Rome, that he was moved to do this by the impulse of Human Nature alone? Who will say it of Quinctius Cincinnatus, who, taken from the plough and made dictator, after the time of office had expired, spontaneously refusing its continuance, followed his plough again? Who will say of Camillus, banished and chased into exile, who, having come to deliver Rome from her enemies, and having accomplished her liberation, spontaneously returned into exile in order not to offend against the authority of the Senate, that he was without Divine inspiration? O, most sacred heart of Cato, who shall presume to speak of thee? Truly, to speak freely of thee is not possible; it were better to be silent and to follow Jerome, when, in the Preface of the Bible where he alludes to Paul, he says that it were better to be silent than say little. Certainly it must be evident, remembering the lives of these men and of the other Divine citizens, that such wonders could not have been without some light of the Divine Goodness, added to their own goodness of nature. And it must be evident that these most excellent men were instruments with which Divine Providence worked in the building up of the Roman Empire, wherein many times the arm of God appeared to be present. And did not God put His own hand to the battle wherein the Albans fought with the Romans in the beginning for the chief dominion, when one Roman alone held in his hands the liberty of Rome? And did not God interfere with His own hands when the Franks, having taken all Rome, attacked by stealth the Capitol by night, and the voice alone of a goose caused this to be known? And did not God interfere with His own hands when, in the war with Hannibal, having lost so many citizens that three bushels of rings were carried into Africa, the Romans wished to abandon the land, if the blessed Scipio the younger had not undertaken his expedition into Africa for the recovery of freedom? And did not God interfere with His own hands when a new citizen of humble station, Tullius, defended, against such a citizen as Catiline, the Roman liberty? Yes, surely. Wherefore one should not need to inquire further to see that an especial birth and an especial success were in the Mind of God decreed to that holy City. And certainly I am of a firm opinion that the stones which remain in her walls are worthy of reverence; and it is asserted and proved that the ground whereon she stands is worthy beyond all other that is occupied by man.

CHAPTER VI.

ABOVE, in the third chapter of this treatise, a promise was made to discourse of the supremacy of the Imperial Authority and of the Philosophic Authority. And since the Imperial Authority has been discussed, my digression must now proceed further in order to consider that of the Philosopher, according to the promise made.

And here we must first see what is the meaning of this word; since here there is a greater necessity to understand it than there was above in the argument on the Imperial Authority, which, on account of its Majesty, does not seem to be doubted. It is then to be known that Authority is no other than the act of the Author.

This word, that is to say, Auctore, without this third letter, *c*, can be derived from two roots. One is from a verb, whose use in grammar is much abandoned, which signifies to bind or to tie words together, that is, A U I E O; and whoso looks well at it in its first vowel or syllable will clearly perceive that it demonstrates it itself, for it is constituted solely of a tie of words, that is, of five vowels alone, which are the soul and bond of every word, and composed of them in a twisted way, to figure the image of a ligature; for beginning with the A, then it twists round into the U, and comes straight through the I into the E, then it revolves and turns round into the O: so that truly this figure represents A, E, I, O, U, which is the figure or form of a tie; and how much *Autore* (Author) derives its origin from this word, one learns from the poets alone, who have bound their words together with the art of harmony; but on this signification we do not at present dwell. The other root from which the word "Autore" (Author) is derived, as Uguccione testifies in the beginning of his Derivations, is a Greek word, "Autentim," which in Latin means "worthy of faith and obedience." And thus "Autore" (Author), derived from this, is taken for any person worthy to be believed and obeyed; and thence comes this word, of which one treats at the present moment, that is to say, Authority. Wherefore one can see that Authority is equivalent to an act worthy of faith and obedience.

[Here is a small break in the original, containing some such words as—Worthy, nay, most worthy, of obedience and of faith is Aristotle:] hence it is evident that his words are a supreme and chief Authority. That Aristotle is most worthy of faith and obedience, one can thus prove. Amongst workmen and artificers of different Arts and Manufactures, which are all directed to one final work of Art, or to one building, the Artificer or Designer of that work must be completely believed in, and implicitly obeyed by all, as the man who alone beholds the ultimate end of all the other ends. Hence the sword-cutler must believe in the knight, so must the bridle-maker and saddle-maker and the shield-maker, and all those trades which are appointed to the profession of knighthood. And since all human actions require an aim, which is that of human life, to which man is appointed inasmuch as he is man, the master and artificer who considers that aim and demonstrates it ought especially to be believed in and obeyed: and he is Aristotle; wherefore he is most worthy of faith and obedience. And in order to see how Aristotle is the master and leader of Human Reason in so far as it aims at its final operation, it is requisite to know that this our aim of life, which each one naturally desires, in most ancient times was searched for by the Wise Men; and since those who desire this end are so numerous, and their desires are as it were all singularly different, although they exist in us universally, it was nevertheless very difficult to discern that end whereon rightly each human appetite or desire might repose.

There were then many ancient philosophers, the first and the chief of whom was Zeno, who saw and believed this end of human life to be solely a rigid honesty, that is to say, rigid without regard to any one in following Truth and Justice, to show no sorrow, to show no joy, to have no sense of any passion whatever. And they defined thus this honest uprightness, as that which, without bearing fruit, is to be praised for reason of itself. And these men and their sect were called Stoics; and that glorious Cato was one of them, of whom in the previous chapter I had not courage enough to speak.

Other philosophers there were who saw and believed otherwise; and of these the first and chief was a philosopher, who was named Epicurus, who, seeing that each animal as soon as it is born is as it were directed by Nature to its right end, which shuns pain and seeks for pleasure, said that this end or aim of ours was enjoyment. I do not say greedy enjoyment, voluntade, but I write it with a *p*, voluptate, that is, delight or pleasure free from pain; and therefore between pleasure and pain no mean was placed. He said that pleasure was no other than no pain; as Tullius seems to say in the first chapter De Finibus. And of these, who from Epicurus are named Epicureans, was Torquatus, a noble Roman, descended from the blood of the glorious Torquatus mention of whom I made above. There were others, and they had their rise from Socrates, and then from his successor, Plato, who, looking more subtly, and seeing that in our actions it was possible to sin, and that one sinned in too much and in too little, said that our action, without excess and without defect, measured to the due mean of our own choice, is virtue, and virtue is the aim of man; and they called it action with virtue. And these were called Academicians, as was Plato and Speusippus, his nephew; they were thus called from the place where Plato taught, that is, the Academy; neither from Socrates did they take or assume any word, because in his Philosophy nothing was affirmed. Truly Aristotle, who had his surname from Stagira, and Xenocrates of Chalcedon, his companion, through the genius, almost Divine, which Nature had put into Aristotle, knowing this end by means of the Socratic method, with the Academic file, as it were, reduced Moral Philosophy to perfection, and especially Aristotle. And since Aristotle began to reason while walking hither and thither, they were called, he, I say, and his companions, Peripatetics, which means the same as walkers about. And since the perfection of this Morality by Aristotle was attained, the name of Academician became extinct, and all those who attached themselves to this sect are called Peripatetics, and these people hold the doctrine of the government of the World through all its parts : and it may be termed a catholic opinion, as it were. Wherefore it is possible to see that Aristotle was the Indicator and the Leader of the people to this mark. And this is what I wished to prove.

Wherefore, collecting all together, the principal intention is manifest, that is to say, that the authority of him whom we understand to be the supreme Philosopher is full of complete vigour, and in no way repugnant to Imperial Authority. But the Imperial without the Philosopher is dangerous ; and this without that is weak, not of itself, but through the disorder of the people : but when one is united with the other they are together most useful and full of all vigour; and therefore it is written in that Book of Wisdom : "Love the Light of Wisdom, all you who are before the people," that is to say, unite Philosophic Authority with the Imperial, in order to rule well and perfectly. O, you miserable ones, who rule at the present time! and O, most miserable ones, you who are ruled! For no Philosophic Authority is united with your governments, neither through suitable study nor by counsel ; so that to all it is possible to repeat those words from Ecclesiastes : "Woe to thee, O land, when thy King is a child, and thy Princes eat in the morning ; " and to no land is it possible to say that which follows : "Blessed art thou, O land, when thy King is the son of nobles, and thy Princes eat in due season, for strength and not for drunkenness."

Ye enemies of God, look to your flanks, ye who have seized the sceptres of the kingdoms of Italy. And I say to you, Charles, and to you, Frederick, Kings, and to you, ye other Princes and Tyrants, see who sits by the side of you in council, and count how many times a day this aim of human life is indicated to you by your councillors. Better would it be for you, like swallows, to fly low down than, like kites, to make lofty circles over carrion.

CHAPTER VII.

Since it is seen how much the Imperial Authority and the Philosophic are to be revered, which must support the opinions propounded, it is now for us to return into the straight path to the intended goal. I say, then, that this last opinion of the Common People has continued so long that without other cause, without inquiry into any reason, every man is termed Noble who may be the son or nephew of any brave man, although he himself is nothing. And this is what the Song says:

> And so long among us
> This falsehood has had sway,
> That men call him a Nobleman,
> Though worthless, who can say,
>
> I nephew am, or son,
> Of one worth such a sum.

Wherefore it is to be observed that it is most dangerous negligence to allow this evil opinion to take root; for even as weeds multiply in the uncultivated field, and surmount and cover the ear of the corn, so that, looking at it from a distance, the wheat appears not, and finally the corn is lost; so the evil opinion in the mind, neither chastised nor corrected, increases and multiplies, so that the ear of Reason, that is, the true opinion, is concealed and buried as it were, and so it is lost. O, how great is my undertaking in this Song, for I wish now to weed the field so full of wild and woody plants as is this field of the common opinion so long bereft of tillage! Certainly I do not intend to cleanse all, but only those parts where the ears of Reason are not entirely overcome; that is, I intend to lift up again those in whom some little light of Reason still lives through the goodness of their nature; the others need only as much care as the brute beasts: wherefore it seems to me that it would not be a less miracle to lead back to Reason him in whom it is entirely extinct than to bring back to Life him who has been four days in the grave.

Then the evil quality of this popular opinion is narrated suddenly, as if it were a horrible thing; it strikes at that, springing forth from the order of the confutation, saying, "But he who sees the Truth will know How vile he has become," in order to make people understand its intolerable wickedness, saying, that those men lie especially, for not only is the man vile, that is, not Noble, who, although descended from good people, is himself wicked, but also he is most vile; and I quote the example of the right path being indicated, where, to prove this, it is fit for me to propound a question, and to reply to that question in this way.

There is a plain with certain paths, a field with hedges, with ditches, with rocks, with tanglewood, with all kinds of obstacles; with the exception of its two straight paths. And it has snowed so much that the snow covers everything, and presents one smooth appearance on every side, so that no trace of any path is to be seen. Here comes a man from one part of the country, and he wishes to go to a house which is on the other side; and by his industry, that is, through prudent foresight and through the goodness of genius, guided solely by himself, he goes through the right path whither he meant to go, leaving the prints of his footsteps behind him. Another comes after this man, and he wishes to go to that mansion, and to him it is only needful to follow the footprints left there; but through his own fault this man strays from the path, which the first man without a guide has known how to keep; this man, though it is pointed out to him, loses his way through the brambles and the rocks, and he goes not to the place whither he is bound.

Which of these men ought to be termed excellent, brave, or worthy? I reply: He who went first. How would you designate that other man? I reply: "As most vile." Why is he not called unworthy or cowardly, that is to say, vile? I reply: Because unworthy, that is, vile, he should be called who, having no guide, might have failed to walk straightforward; but since this man had a guide, his error and his fault can rise higher; and therefore he is to be called, not vile, but most vile. And likewise he who, by his father or by some elder of his race is ennobled, and does not continue in a noble course, not only is he vile, but he is most vile, and deserving of as much contempt and infamy as any other villain, if not of more. And because a man may preserve himself from this vile baseness, Solomon lays this command on him who has had a brave and excellent ancestor, in the twenty-second chapter of Proverbs: "Remove not the ancient landmark, which thy fathers have set." And previously he says, in the fourth chapter of the said book: "The path of the Just," that is, of the worthy men, "is as the shining light, that shineth more and more unto the perfect day; the way of the wicked is as darkness, and they know not at what they stumble."

Finally, when it says, "And though he walks upon the earth Is counted with the dead," to his greater disgrace I say that this most worthless man is dead, seeming still alive. Where it is to be known that the wicked man may be truly said to be dead, and especially he who goes astray from the path trodden by his good ancestor. And this it is possible to prove thus: as Aristotle says in the second book On the Soul, to live is to be with the living; and since there are many ways of living—as in the plants to vegetate; in the animals to vegetate and to feel and to move; in men to vegetate, to feel, to move, and to reason, or rather to understand; and since things ought to be denominated by the noblest part, it is evident that in animals to live is to feel—in the brute animals, I say; in man, to live is to use reason. Wherefore, if to live is the life or existence of man, and if thus to depart from the use of Reason, which is his life, is to depart from life or existence, even thus is that man dead.

And does he not depart from the use of Reason who does not reason or think concerning the aim of his life? And does he not depart from the use of Reason who does not reason or think concerning the path which he ought to take? Certainly he does so depart; and this is evident especially in him who has the footprints before him, and looks not at them; and therefore Solomon says in the fifth chapter of Proverbs: "He shall die without instruction; and in the greatness of his folly he shall go astray," that is to say, he is dead who becomes a disciple, and who does not follow his master; and such an one is most vile.

And of him it would be possible for some one to say: How is he dead and yet he walks? I reply, that as a man he is dead, but as a beast he has remained alive; for as the Philosopher says in the second book On the Soul, the powers of the Soul stand upon itself, as the figure of the quadrangle stands upon the triangle, and the pentagon stands upon the quadrangle; so the sensitive stands upon the vegetative, and the intellectual stands upon the sensitive. Wherefore, as, by removing the last side of the pentagon, the quadrangle remains, so by removing the last power of the Soul, that is, Reason, the man no longer remains, but a thing with a sensitive soul only, that is, the brute animal.

And this is the meaning or intention of the second part of the devised Song, in which are placed the opinions of others.

CHAPTER VIII.

THE most beautiful branch which grows up from the root of Reason is Discretion. For as St. Thomas says thereupon in the prologue to the book of Ethics, to know the order of one thing to another is the proper act of Reason; and this is Discretion. One of the most beautiful and sweetest fruits of this

The Fourth Treatise.

SOFT rhymes of love I used to find
    Within my thought, I now must leave,
Not without hope to turn to them again ;
    But signs of a disdainful mind
        That in my Lady I perceive
Have closed the way to my accustomed strain.

    And since time suits me now to wait,
        I put away the softer style
Proper to love ; rhyme subtle and severe
    Shall tell how Nobleman's estate
        Is won by worth, hold false and vile
The judgment that from wealth derives a Peer.

        First calling on that Lord
            Who dwells within her eyes,
        Containing whom, my Lady learnt
            Herself to love and prize.

        One raised to Empire held,
            As far as he could see,
        Descent of wealth, and generous ways,
            To make Nobility.

        Another, lightly wise,
            That saying turned aside,
        Perchance for want of generous ways
            The second source denied.

        And followers of him
            Are all the men who rate
        Those noble in whose families
            The wealth has long been great.

And so long among us
   The falsehood has had sway,
That men call him a Nobleman,
   Though worthless, who can say,

I nephew am, or son,
   Of one worth such a sum;
But he who sees the Truth may know
   How vile he has become

To whom the Truth was shown,
   Who from the Truth has fled,
And though he walks upon the earth
   Is counted with the dead :

Whoever shall define
   The man a living tree
Will speak untruth and less than truth,
   Though more he may not see.

The Emperor so erred ;
   First set the false in view,
Proceeding, on the other side,
   To what was less than true.

For riches make not worth
   Although they can defile ;
Nor can their want take worth away :
   They are by nature vile.

No painter gives a form
   That is not of his knowing ;
No tower leans above a stream
   That far away is flowing.

How vile and incomplete
   Wealth is, let this declare
However great the heap may be
   It brings no peace, but care.

And hence the upright mind,
   To its own purpose true,
Stands firm although the flood of wealth
   Sweep onward out of view.

They will not have the vile
  Turn noble, nor descent
From parent vile produce a race
  For ever eminent.

Yet this, they say, can be,
  Their reason halts behind,
Since time they suit to noble birth
  By course of time defined.

It follows then from this
  That all are high or base,
Or that in Time there never was
  Beginning to our race.

But that I cannot hold,
  Nor yet, if Christians, they;
Sound intellect reproves their words
  As false, and turns away.

And now I seek to tell,
  As it appears to me,
What is, whence comes, what signs attest
  A true Nobility.

I say that from one root
  Each Virtue firstly springs,
Virtue, I mean, that Happiness
  To man, by action, brings.

This, as the Ethics teach,
  Is habit of right choice
That holds the means between extremes,
  So spake that noble voice.

Nobility by right
  No other sense has had
Than to import its subject's good,
  As vileness makes him bad.

Such virtue shows its good
  To others' intellect,
For when two things agree in one,
  Producing one effect.

One must from other come,
   Or each one from a third,
If each be as each, and more, then one
   From the other is inferred.

Where Virtue is, there is
   A Nobleman, although
Not where there is a Nobleman
   Must Virtue be also.

So likewise that is Heaven
   Wherein a star is hung,
But Heaven may be starless; so
   In women and the young

A modesty is seen,
   Not virtue, noble yet;
Comes virtue from what's noble, as
   From black comes violet;

Or from the parent root
   It springs, as said before,
And so let no one vaunt that him
   A noble mother bore.

They are as Gods whom Grace
   Has placed beyond all sin:
God only gives it to the Soul
   That He finds pure within.

That seed of Happiness
   Falls in the hearts of few,
Planted by God within the Souls
   Spread to receive His dew.

Souls whom this Grace adorns
   Declare it in each breath,
From birth that joins the flesh and soul
   They show it until death.

In Childhood they obey,
   Are gentle, modest, heed
To furnish Virtue's person with
   The graces it may need.

branch is the reverence which the lesser owes to the greater. Wherefore Tullius, in the first chapter of the Offices, when speaking of the beauty which shines forth in Uprightness, says that reverence is part of that beauty; and thus as this reverence is the beauty of Uprightness, so its opposite is baseness and want of uprightness; which opposite quality it is possible to term irreverence, or rather as impudent boldness, in our Vulgar Tongue.

And therefore this Tullius in the same place says: "To treat with contemptuous indifference that which others think of one, not only is the act of an arrogant, but also of a dissolute person," which means no other except that arrogance and dissolute conduct show want of self-knowledge, which is the beginning of the capacity for all reverence. Wherefore I, desiring (and bearing meanwhile all reverence both to the Prince and to the Philosopher) to remove the infirmity from the minds of some men, in order afterwards to build up thereupon the light of truth, before I proceed to confute the opinions propounded, will show how, whilst confuting those opinions, I argue with irreverence neither against the Imperial Majesty nor against the Philosopher. For if in any part of this entire book I should appear irreverent, it would not be so bad as in this treatise; in which, whilst treating of Nobility, I ought to appear Noble, and not vile.

And firstly I will prove that I do not presume against the authority of the Philosopher; then I will prove that I do not presume against Imperial Majesty.

I say, then, that when the Philosopher says, "that which appears to the most is impossible to be entirely false," I do not mean to speak of the external appearance, that is, the sensual, but of that which appears within, the rational; since the sensual appearance, according to most people, is many times most false, especially in the common things appreciable by the senses, wherein the sense is often deceived. Thus we know that to most people the Sun appears of the width of a foot in diameter; and this is most false, for, according to the inquiry and the discovery which human reason has made with its skill, the diameter of the body of the Sun is five times as much as that of the Earth and also one-half time more, since the Earth in its diameter is six thousand five hundred miles, the diameter of the Sun, which to the sense of sight presents the appearance of the width of one foot, is thirty-five thousand seven hundred and fifty miles. Wherefore it is evident that Aristotle did not understand or judge it by the appearance which it presents to the sense of sight. And therefore, if I intend only to oppose false trust in appearance according to the senses, that is not done against the intention of the Philosopher, and therefore I do not offend against the reverence which is due to him.

And that I intend to confute the appearance according to the sense is manifest; for those people who judge thus, judge only by what they feel or think of those things which fortune can give and take away. For, because they see great alliances made and high marriages to take place, and the wonderful palaces, the large possessions, great lordships, they believe that all those things are the causes of Nobility—nay, they believe them to be Nobility itself. For if they could judge with any appearance of reason, they would say the contrary, that is, that Nobility is the cause of these things, as will be seen in the sequel of this treatise. And even as it may be seen that I speak not against the reverence due to the Philosopher whilst confuting this error, so I speak not against the reverence due to the Empire; and the reason I intend to show. But when he reasons or argues before the adversary, the Rhetorician ought to use much caution in his speech, in order that the adversary may not derive thence material wherewith to disturb the Truth. I, who speak in this treatise in the presence of so many adversaries, cannot speak briefly; wherefore, if my digressions should be long, let no one marvel.

I say, then, that, in order to prove that I am not irreverent to the Majesty of the Empire, it is requisite, in the first place, to see what reverence is. I say that reverence is no other than a confession of due submission by an evident sign; and, having seen this, it remains to distinguish between them. Irreverent expresses privation, not reverent expresses negation; and, therefore, irreverence is to disavow the due submission by a manifest sign. The want of reverence is to refuse submission as not due. A man can deny or refuse a thing in a double sense. In one way, the man can deny offending against the Truth when he abstains from the due confession, and this properly is to disavow. In another way, the man can deny offending against the Truth when he does not confess that which is not, and this is proper negation; even as for the man to deny that he is entirely mortal is to deny properly speaking. Wherefore, if I deny or refuse reverence due to the Imperial Authority, I am not irreverent, but I am not reverent; which is not against reverence, forasmuch as it offends not that Imperial Authority; even as not to live does not offend Life, but Death, which is privation of that Life, offends; wherefore, to die is one thing and not to live is another thing, for not to live is in the stones. And since Death expresses privation, which cannot be except in decease of the subject, and the stones are not the subject of Life, they should not be called dead, but not living. In like manner, I, who in this case ought not to have reverence to the Imperial Authority, am not irreverent if I deny or refuse it, but I am not reverent, which is neither boldness, nor presumption, nor a thing to be blamed. But it would be presumption to be reverent, if it could be called reverence, since it would fall into greater and more true irreverence, that is, into irreverence of Nature and of Truth, as will be seen in the sequel. Against this error that Master of Philosophers, Aristotle, guards, in the beginning of the book of Ethics, when he says: "If the friends are two, and one is the Truth, their one mind is the Truth's." If I have said that I am not reverent, that is, to deny reverence, or by a manifest sign to deny or refuse a submission not due. It is to be seen how this is to deny and not to disavow, that is to say, it remains to be seen how, in this case, I am not rightfully subject to the Imperial Majesty. It must be a long argument wherewith I intend to prove this in the chapter next following.

CHAPTER IX.

To see how in this case, that is, in approving or in not approving the opinion of the Emperor, I am not held in subjection to him, it is necessary to recall to mind that which has been argued previously concerning the Imperial Office, in the fourth chapter of this treatise, namely, that to promote the perfection of human Life, Imperial Authority was designed; and that it is the director and ruler of all our operations, and justly so, for however far our operations extend themselves, so far the Imperial Majesty has jurisdiction, and beyond those limits it does not reach. But as each Art and Office of mankind is restricted by the Imperial Office within certain limits, so this Imperial Office is confined by God within certain bounds. And it is not to be wondered at, for the Office and the Arts of Nature in all her operations we see to be limited. For if we wish to take Universal Nature, it has jurisdiction as far as the whole World, I say as far as Heaven and Earth extend; and this within a certain limit, as is proved by the third chapter of the book on Physics, and by the first chapter, of Heaven and the World. Then the jurisdiction of Univeral Nature is limited within a certain boundary, and consequently the individual; of which also He is the Limiter who is limited by nothing, that is, the First Goodness, that is, God, who alone with infinite capacity comprehends the Infinite. And, that we may see the limits of our operations, it is to be known that those alone are our operations which are subject to Reason and to Will; for, if in us there is the digestive operation, that is not human, but natural.

And it is to be known that our Reason is ordained to four operations, separately to be considered; for those are operations which Reason only considers and does not produce, neither can produce, any one of them, such as are the Natural facts and the Supernatural and the Mathematics. And those are operations which it considers and does in its own proper act which are called rational, such as are the arts of speech. And those are operations which it considers and does in material beyond itself, such as are the Mechanical Arts. And all these operations, although the considering them is subject to our will, they in their essential form are not subject to our will; for although we might will that heavy things should mount upwards naturally, they would not be able to ascend; and although we might will that the syllogism with false premisses should conclude with demonstration of the Truth, it could not so conclude; and although we might will that the house should stand as firmly when leaning forward as when upright, it could not be; since of those operations we are not properly the factors, we are their discoverers; Another ordained them and made them, the great Maker, who alone can Will and Do All—God.

There also are operations which our Reason considers and which lie in the act of the Will, such as to offend and to rejoice; such as to stand firm in the battle and to fly from it; such as to be chaste and to be lewd; these are entirely subject to our will, and therefore we are called from them good and evil, because such acts are entirely our own; for so far as our will can obtain power, so far do our operations extend. And since in all these voluntary operations there is some equity to preserve and some iniquity to shun—which equity may be lost through two causes, either through not knowing what it is, or through not wishing to follow it—the written Reason, the Law, was invented, both to point it out to us and to command its observance. Wherefore Augustine says: "If men could know this, that is, Equity, and knowing it would obey it, the written Reason, the Law, would not be needful." And therefore it is written in the beginning of the old Digests or Books of the Civil Law: "The written Reason is the Art of Goodness and of Equity." To write this, to show forth and to enforce this, is the business of that Official Post of which one speaks, that of the Emperor, to whom, as has been said, in so far as our own operations extend, we are subject, and no farther. For this reason in each Art and in each trade the artificers and the scholars are and ought to be subject to the chief and to the master of their trades and Art; beyond their callings the subjection ceases, because the superiority ceases. So that it is possible to speak of the Emperor in this manner, if we will represent his office figuratively, and say that he may be the rider of the Human Will, of which horse how it goes without its rider through the field is evident enough, and especially in miserable Italy, left without any means for its right government. And it is considered that in proportion as a thing is more fit for the Master's art, so much the greater is the subjection; for the cause being multiplied, so is the effect multiplied. Wherefore it is to be known that there are things which are such pure or simple Arts that Nature is their instrument; even as rowing with an oar, where the Art makes its instrument by impulsion, which is a natural movement; as in the threshing of the corn, where the Art makes its instrument, which is a natural quality.

And in this especially a man ought to be subject to the chief and master of the Art. And there are things in which Art is the instrument of Nature, and these are lesser Arts; and in these the artificers are less subject to their chief, as in giving the seed to the Earth, where one must await the will of Nature; as to sail out of the harbour or port, where one must await the natural disposition of the weather; and therefore we often see in these things contention amongst the artificers, and the greater to ask counsel of the lesser. And there are other things which are not Arts, but appear to have some relationship with them; and therefore men are often deceived; and in these the scholars are not subject to a master, neither are they bound to believe in him so far as regards the Art. Thus, to fish seems to have some relationship with navigation; and to know the virtue of the herb or grass seems to have some relationship with agriculture; for these Arts have no general rule, since fishing may be below the Art of hunting, and beneath its command; to know the virtue of the herb may be below the science of medicine, or rather below its most noble teaching.

Those things which have been argued concerning the other Arts in like manner may be seen in the Imperial Art, for there are rules in those Arts which are pure or simple Arts, as are the laws of marriage, of servants, of armies, of successors in offices of dignity; and in all these we may be entirely subject to the Emperor without doubt and without any suspicion whatever. There are other laws which are the followers of Nature, such as to constitute a man of sufficient age to fill some office in the administration; and to such a law as this we are entirely subject; there are many others which appear to have some relationship with the Imperial Art; and here he was and is deceived who believes that the Imperial judgment in this part may be authentic, as of youth, whose nature is laid down by no Imperial judgment, as it were, of the Emperor. Render, therefore, unto God that which is God's. Wherefore it is not to be believed, nor to be allowed, because it was said by Nero the Emperor that youth is beauty and strength of body; but credit would be given to the philosopher who should say that youth is the crown or summit of the natural life. And therefore it is evident that to define Nobility is not the function of the Art Imperial; and if it is not in the nature of the Art, when we are treating of Nobility we are not subject to it; and if we are not subject, we are not bound to yield reverence therein; and this is the conclusion we have sought.

Now, therefore, with all freedom, with all liberty of mind, it remains to strike to the heart the vicious opinions, thereby causing them to fall to earth, in order that the Truth by means of this my victory may hold the field in the mind of him for whom it is good that this Light should shine clear.

CHAPTER X.

SINCE the opinions of others concerning Nobility have now been brought forward, and since it has been shown that it is lawful for me to confute those opinions, I shall now proceed to discourse concerning that part of the Song which confutes those opinions, beginning, as has been said above: "Whoever shall define 'The man a living tree.'" And therefore it it to be known that in the opinion of the Emperor, although it states it defectively in one part, that is, where he spoke of "generous ways," he alluded to the manners of the Nobility; and therefore the Song does not intend to reprove that part: the other part, which is entirely opposed to the nature of Nobility, it does intend to confute, which cites two things when it says: "Descent of wealth," "The wealth has long been great," that is, time and riches, which are entirely apart from Nobility, as has been said, and as will be shown farther on; and, therefore, in this confutation two divisions are made: in the first we deny the Nobility of riches, then confute the idea that time can cause Nobility. The second part begins: "They will not have the vile Turn noble."

It is to be known that, riches being reproved, not only is the opinion of the Emperor reproved in that part which alludes to the riches, but also entirely that opinion of the common people, which was founded solely upon riches. The first part is divided into two: in the first it says in a general way that the Emperor was erroneous in his definition of Nobility; secondly, it shows the reason why or how that is; and this begins that second part, "For riches make no Nobleman."

I say, then, "Whoever shall define The man a living tree," that, firstly, he will speak untruth, inasmuch as he says "tree," and "less than truth," inasmuch as he says "living," and does not say rational, which is the difference whereby Man is distinguished from the Beast. Then I say that in this way he was erroneous in his definition, he who held Imperial Office, not saying Emperor, but "one raised to Empire," to indicate, as has been said above, that this question is beyond the bounds of the Imperial Office. In like manner I say that he errs who places a false subject under Nobility, that is, "descent of wealth," and then proceeds to a defective form, or rather difference, that is, "generous ways," which do not contain any essential part of Nobility, but only a small part, as will appear below. And it is not to be omitted, although the text may be silent, that my Lord the Emperor in this part did not err in the parts of the definition, but only in the mode of the definition, although, according to what fame reports of him, he was a logician and a great scholar; that is to say, the definition of Nobility can be made more sufficiently by the effects than by the principles or premisses, since it appears to have the place of a first principle or premiss, which it is not possible to notify by first things, but by subsequent things. Then, when I say, "For riches make not worth," I show how they cannot possibly be the cause of Nobility, because they are vile. And I prove that they have not the power to take it away, because they are disjoined so much from Nobility. And I prove these to be vile by an especial and most evident defect; and I do this when I say, "How vile and incomplete." Finally, I conclude, by virtue of that which is said above:

> And hence the upright mind,
>   To its own purpose true,
> Stands firm although the flood of wealth
>   Sweep onward out of view;

which proves that which is said above, that those riches are disunited from Nobility by not following the effect of union with it. Where it is to be known that, as the Philosopher expresses it, all the things which make anything must first exist perfectly within the being of the thing out of which that other thing is made. Wherefore he says in the seventh chapter of the Metaphysics: "When one thing is generated from another, it is generated of that thing by being in that Being."

Again, it is to be known that each thing which becomes corrupt is thus corrupted by some change or alteration, and each thing which is changed or altered must be conjoined with the cause of the change, even as the Philosopher expresses it in the seventh chapter of the book on Physics and in the first chapter on Generation. These things being propounded, I proceed thus, and I say that riches, as another man believed, cannot possibly bestow Nobility, and to prove how great is the difference between them I say that they are unable to take Nobility away from him who possesses it. To bestow it they have not the power, since by nature they are vile, and because of their vileness they are opposed to Nobility. And here by vileness one means baseness, through degeneracy, which is directly opposite to Nobility: for the one opposite thing cannot be the maker of the other, neither is it possible to be, for the reason given above, which is briefly added to the text, saying, "No painter gives a form That is not of his knowing." Wherefore no painter would be able to depict any figure or form if he could not first design what such figure or form ought to be.

Again, riches cannot take it away, because they are so far from Nobility; and, for the reason previously narrated, that which alters or corrupts anything must be conjoined with that thing, and therefore it is subjoined: "No tower leans above a stream That far away is flowing," which means nothing more than to accord with that which has been previously said, that riches cannot take Nobility away, saying that Nobility is, as it were, an upright tower and riches a river flowing swiftly in the distance.

CHAPTER XI.

It now remains only to prove how vile riches are, and how disjoined and far apart they are from Nobility; and this is proved in two little parts of the text, to which at present it is requisite to pay attention, and then, those being explained, what I have said will be evident, namely, that riches are vile and far apart from Nobility, and hereby the reasons stated above against riches will be perfectly proved.

I say then, "How vile and incomplete Wealth is," and to make evident what I intend to say it is to be known that the vileness or baseness of each thing is derived from the imperfection of that thing, and Nobility from its perfection: wherefore in proportion as a thing is perfect, it is noble in its nature; in proportion as it is imperfect, it is vile. And therefore, if riches are imperfect, it is evident that they are vile or base. And that they are imperfect, the text briefly proves when it says: "However great the heap may be, It brings no peace, but care;" in which it is evident, not only that they are imperfect, but most imperfect, and therefore they are most vile; and Lucan bears witness to this when he says, speaking of those same riches: "Without strife or contention or opposition, the Laws would perish, and you, Riches, the basest part of things, you move or are the cause of Battles." It is possible briefly to see their imperfection in three things quite clearly: firstly, in the indiscriminate manner in which they fall to a person's lot; secondly, in their dangerous increase; thirdly, in their hurtful possession.

And, firstly, that which I demonstrate concerning this is to clear up a doubt which seems to arise, for, since gold, pearls, and lands, may have in their essential being perfect form and act, it does not seem true to say that they are imperfect. And therefore one must distinguish that inasmuch as by themselves, of them it is considered, they are perfect things, and they are not riches, but gold and pearls; but inasmuch as they are appointed to the possession of man they are riches, and in this way they are full of imperfection; which is not an unbecoming or impossible thing, considered from different points of view, to be perfect and imperfect. I say that their imperfection firstly may be observed in the indiscretion, or unwisdom, or folly, of their arrival, in which no distributive Justice shines forth, but complete iniquity almost always; which iniquity is the proper effect of imperfection. For if the methods or ways by which they come are considered, all may be gathered together in three methods, or kinds of ways: for, either they come by simple chance, as when without intention or hope they come upon some discovery not thought of; or they come by fortune which is aided by law or right, as by will, or testament, or succession; or they come by fortune, the helper of the Law, as by lawful or unlawful provision; lawful, I say, when by art, or skill, or by trade, or deserved kindness; unlawful, I say, when either by theft or rapine. And in each one of these three ways, one sees that inequitable character of which I speak, for more often to the wicked than to the good the hidden treasures which are discovered present themselves; and this is so evident, that it has no need of proof. I saw the place in the side of a hill, or mountain, in Tuscany, which is called Falterona, where the most vile peasant of all the country, whilst digging, found more than a bushel of the finest Santèlena silver, which had awaited him perhaps for more than a thousand years. And in order to see this iniquity, Aristotle said that in proportion as the Man is subject to the Intellect, so much the less is he the slave of Fortune. And I say that oftener to the wicked than to the good befall legal inheritance and property by succession; and concerning this I do not wish to bring forward any proof, but let each one turn his eyes round his own immediate neighbourhood, and he will see that concerning which I am silent that I may not offend or bring shame to some one. Would to God that might be which was demanded by the Man of Provence, namely, that the man who is not the heir of goodness should lose the inheritance of wealth. And I say that many times to the wicked more than to the good comes rich provision, for the unlawful never comes to the good, because they refuse it; and what good man ever would endeavour to enrich himself by force or fraud? That would be impossible, for by the mere choice of the enterprise he would no more be good. And the lawful gains of wealth but rarely fall to the lot of the good, because, since much anxiety or anxious care is required therein, and the solicitude of the good is directed to greater things, the good man is rarely solicitous enough to seek them. Wherefore it is evident that in each way these riches fall unjustly or inequitably; and therefore our Lord called them wicked or unrighteous when He said, "Make to yourselves friends of the Mammon of unrighteousness," inviting and encouraging men to be liberal with good gifts, which are the begetters of friends. And what a beautiful exchange he makes who gives freely of these most imperfect things in order to have and to acquire perfect things, such as are the hearts of good and worthy men! This exchange it is possible to make every day. Certainly this is a new commerce, different from the others, which, thinking to win one man by generosity, has won thereby thousands and thousands. Who lives not again in the heart of Alexander because of his royal beneficence? Who lives not again in the good King of Castile, or Saladin, or the good Marquis of Monferrat, or the good Count of Toulouse, or Beltramo dal Bornio, or Galasso da Montefeltro, when mention is made of their noble acts of courtesy and liberality? Certainly not only those who would do the same willingly, had they the power, but those even who would die before they would do it, bear love to the memory of these good men.

CHAPTER XII.

As has been said, it is possible to see the imperfection of riches not only in their indiscriminate advent, but also in their dangerous increase; and that in this we may perceive their defect more clearly, the text makes mention of it, saying of those riches, "However great the heap may be It brings no peace, but care;" they create more thirst and render increase more defective and insufficient. And here it is requisite to know that defective things may fail in such a way that on the surface they appear complete, but, under pretext of perfection, the shortcoming is concealed. But they may have those defects so entirely revealed that the imperfection is seen openly on the surface. And those things which do not reveal their defects in the first place are the most dangerous, since very often it is not possible to be on guard against them; even as we see in the traitor who, before our face, shows himself friendly, so that he causes us to have faith in him, and under pretext of friendship, hides the defect of his hostility. And in this way riches, in their increase, are dangerously imperfect, for, submitting to our eyes this that they promise, they bring just the contrary. The treacherous gains always promise that, if collected up to a certain amount, they will make the collector full of every satisfaction; and with this promise they lead the Human Will into the vice of Avarice. And, for this reason, Boëthius calls them, in his book of Consolations, dangerous, saying, "Oh, alas! who was that first man who dug up the precious stones that wished to hide themselves, and who dug out the loads of gold once covered by the hills, dangerous treasures?"

The treacherous ones promise, if we will but look, to remove every want, to quench all thirst, to bring satisfaction and sufficiency; and this they do to every man in the beginning, confirming promise to a certain point in their increase, and then, as soon as their pile rises, in place of contentment and refreshment they bring on an intolerable fever-thirst; and beyond sufficiency, they extend their limit, create a desire to amass more, and, with this, fear and anxiety far in excess of the new gain.

Then, truly, they bring no peace, but more care, more trouble, than a man had in the first place when he was without them. And therefore Tullius says, in that book on Paradoxes, when execrating riches: "I at no time firmly believed the money of those men, or magnificent mansions, or riches, or lordships, or voluptuous joys, with which especially they are shackled, to be amongst things good or desirable, since I saw certain men in the abundance of them especially desire those wherein they abounded; because at no time is the thirst of cupidity quenched; not only are they tormented by the desire for the increase of those things which they possess, but also they have torment in the fear of losing them." And all these are the words of Tullius, and even thus they stand in that book which has been mentioned.

And, as a stronger witness to this imperfection, hear Boëthius, speaking in his book of Consolation: "If the Goddess of Riches were to expand and multiply riches till they were as numerous as the sands thrown up by the sea when tost by the tempest, or countless as the stars that shine, still Man would weep."

And because still further testimony is needful to reduce this to a proof, note how much Solomon and his father David exclaim against them, how much against them is Seneca, especially when writing to Lucilius, how much Horace, how much Juvenal, and, briefly, how much every writer, every poet, and how much Divine Scripture. All Truthful cries aloud against these false enticers to sin, full of all defect. Call to mind also, in aid of faith, what your own eyes have seen, what is the life of those men who follow after riches, how far they live securely when they have piled them up, what their contentment is, how peacefully they rest.

What else daily endangers and destroys cities, countries, individual persons, so much as the fresh heaping up of wealth in the possession of some man? His accumulation wakens new desires, to the fulfilment of which it is not possible to attain without injury to some one.

And what else does the Law, both Canonical and Civil, intend to rectify except cupidity or avarice, which grows with its heaps of riches, and which the Law seeks to resist or prevent. Truly, the Canonical and the Civil Law make it sufficiently clear, if the first sections of their written word are read. How evident it is, nay, I say it is most evident, that these riches are, in their increase, entirely imperfect; when, being amassed, naught else but imperfection can possibly spring forth from them. And this is what the text says.

But here arises a doubtful question, which is not to be passed over without being put and answered. Some calumniator of the Truth might be able to say that if, by increasing desire in their acquisition, riches are imperfect and therefore vile, for this reason science or knowledge is imperfect and vile, in the acquisition of which the desire steadily increases, wherefore Seneca says, "If I should have one foot in the grave, I should still wish to learn."

But it is not true that knowledge is vile through imperfection. By distinction of the consequences, increase of desire is not in knowledge the cause of vileness. That it is perfect is evident, for the Philosopher, in the sixth book of the Ethics, says that science or knowledge is the perfect reason of certain things. To this question one has to reply briefly; but in the first place it is to be seen whether in the acquisition of Knowledge the desire for it is enlarged in the way suggested by the question, and whether the argument be rational. Wherefore I say that not only in the acquisition of knowledge and riches, but in each and every acquisition, human desire expands, although in different ways; and the reason is this: that the supreme desire of each thing bestowed by Nature in the first place is to return to its first source. And since God is the First Cause of our Souls, and the Maker of them after His Own Image, as it is written, "Let us make Man in Our Image, after Our likeness," the Soul especially desires to return to that First Cause. As a pilgrim, who goes along a path where he never journeyed before, may believe every house that he sees in the distance to be his inn, and, not finding it to be so, may direct his belief to the next, and so travel on from house to house until he reach the inn, even so our Soul, as soon as it enters the untrodden path of this life, directs its eyes to its supreme good, the sum of its day's travel to good; and therefore whatever thing it sees which seems to have in itself some goodness, it thinks to be the supreme good. And because its knowledge at first is imperfect, owing to want of experience and want of instruction, good things that are but little appear great to it; and therefore in the first place it begins to desire those. So we see little children desire above all things an apple; and then, growing older, they desire a little bird; and then, being older, desire a beautiful garment; and then a horse, and then a wife, and then moderate wealth, and then greater wealth, and then still more. And this happens because in none of these things that is found for which search is made, and as we live on we seek further. Wherefore it is possible to see that one desirable thing stands under the other in the eyes of our Soul in a way almost pyramidal, for the least first covers the whole, and is as it were the point of the desirable good, which is God, at the basis of all; so that the farther it proceeds from the point towards the basis, so much the greater do the desirable good things appear; and this is the reason why, by acquisition, human desires become broader the one after the other.

But, thus this pathway is lost through error, even as in the roads of the earth; for as from one city to another there is of necessity an excellent direct road, and often another which branches from that, the branch road goes into another part, and of many others some do not go all the way, and some go farther round; so in Human Life there are different roads, of which one is the truest, and another the most misleading, and some are less right, and some less wrong. And as we see that the straightest road to the city satisfies desire and gives rest after toil, and that which goes in the opposite direction never satisfies and never can give rest, so it happens in our Life. The man who follows the right path attains his end, and gains his rest. The man who follows the wrong path never attains it, but with much fatigue of mind and greedy eyes looks always before him.

Wherefore, although this argument does not entirely reply to the question asked above, at least it opens the way to the reply, which causes us to see that each desire of ours does not proceed in its expansion in one way alone. But because this chapter is somewhat prolonged, we will reply in a new chapter to the question, wherein may be ended the whole disputation which it is our intention to make against riches.

CHAPTER XIII.

IN reply to the question, I say that it is not possible to affirm properly that the desire for knowledge does increase, although, as has been said, it does expand in a certain way. For that which properly increases is always one; the desire for knowledge is not always one, but is many; and one desire fulfilled, another comes; so that, properly speaking, its expansion is not its increase, but it is advance of a succession of smaller things into great things. For if I desire to know the principles of natural things, as soon as I know these, that desire is satisfied and there is an end of it. If I then desire to know the why and the wherefore of each one of these principles, this is a new desire altogether. Nor by the advent of that new desire am I deprived of the perfection to which the other might lead me. Such an expansion as that is not the cause of imperfection, but of new perfection. That expansion of riches, however, is properly increased which is always one, so that no succession is seen therein, and therefore no end and no perfection.

And if the adversary would say, that if the desire to know the first principles of natural things is one thing, and the desire to know what they are is another, so is the desire for a hundred marks one thing, and the desire for a thousand marks is another, I reply that it is not true; for the hundred is part of the thousand and is related to it, as part of a line to the whole of the line along which one proceeds by one impulse alone; and there is no succession there, nor completion of motion in any part. But to know what the principles of natural things are is not the same as to know what each one of them is; the one is not part of the other, and they are related to each other as diverging lines along which one does not proceed by one impulse, but the completed movement of the one succeeds the completed movement of the other. And thus it appears that, because of the desire for knowledge, knowledge is not to be called imperfect in the same way as riches are to be called imperfect, on account of the desire for them, as the question put it; for in the desire for knowledge the desires terminate successively with the attainment of their aims; and in the desire for riches, NO; so that the question is solved.

Again, the adversary may calumniate, saying that, although many desires are fulfilled in the acquisition of knowledge, the last is never attained, which is the imperfection of that one desire, which does not gain its end; and that will be both one and imperfect.

Again one here replies that it is not a truth which is brought forward in opposition, that is, that the last desire is never attained; for our natural desires, as is proved in the third treatise of this book, are all tending to a certain end; and the desire for knowledge is natural, so that this desire compasses a certain end, although but few, since they walk in the wrong path, accomplish the day's journey. And he who understands the Commentator in the third chapter, On the Soul, learns this of him; and therefore Aristotle says, in the tenth chapter of the Ethics, against Simonides the Poet, that man ought to draw near to Divine things as much as is possible; wherein he shows that our power tends towards a certain end. And in the first book of the Ethics he says that the disciplined Mind demands certainty in its knowledge of things in proportion as their nature received certainty, in which he proves that not only on the side of the man desiring knowledge, but on the side of the desired object of knowledge, attention ought to be given; and therefore St. Paul says: "Not much knowledge, but right knowledge in moderation." So that in whatever way the desire for knowledge is considered, either generally or particularly, it comes to perfection.

And since knowledge is a noble perfection, and through the desire for it its perfection is not lost, as is the case with the accursed riches, we must note briefly how injurious they are when possessed, and this is the third notice of their imperfection. It is possible to see that the possession of them is injurious for two reasons: one, that it is the cause of evil; the other, that it is the privation of good. It is the cause of evil, which makes the timid possessor wakeful, watchful, and suspicious or hateful.

How great is the fear of that man who knows he carries wealth about him, when walking abroad, when dwelling at home, when not only wakeful or watching, but when sleeping, not only the fear that he may lose his property, but fear for his life because he possesses these riches! Well do the miserable merchants know, who travel through the World, that the leaves which the wind stirs on the trees cause them to tremble when they are bearing their wealth with them; and when they are without it, full of confidence they go singing and talking, and thus make their journey shorter! Therefore the Wise

Man says: "If the traveller enters on his road empty, he can sing in the presence of thieves." And this Lucan desires to express in the fifth book, when he praises the safety of poverty: "O, the safe and secure liberty of the poor Life! O, narrow dwelling-places and thrift! O, not again deem riches to be of the Gods! In what temples and within what palace walls could this be, that is to have no fear, in some tumult or other, of striking the hand of Cæsar?"

And Lucan says this when he depicts how Cæsar came by night to the little house of the fisher Amyclas to cross the Adriatic Sea. And how great is the hatred that each man bears to the possessor of riches, either through envy, or from the desire to take possession of his wealth! So true it is, that often and often, contrary to due filial piety, the son meditates the death of the father; and most great and most evident experience of this the Italians can have, both on the banks of the Po and on the banks of the Tiber. And therefore Boëthius in the second chapter of his Consolations says: "Certainly Avarice makes men hateful."

Nay, their possession is privation of good, for, possessing those riches, a man does not give freely with generosity, which is a virtue, which is a perfect good, and which makes men magnificent and beloved; which does not lie in possession of those riches, but in ceasing to possess them. Wherefore Boëthius in the same book says: "Then money is good when, bartered for other things, by the use of generosity one no longer possesses it." Wherefore the baseness of riches is sufficiently proved by all these remarks of his; and therefore the man with an upright desire and true knowledge never loves them;

and, not loving them, he does not unite himself to them, but always desires them to be far from himself, except inasmuch as they are appointed to some necessary service ; and it is a reasonable thing, since the perfect cannot be united with the imperfect. So we see that the curved line never joins the straight line, and if there be any conjunction, it is not of line to line, but of point to point. And thus it follows that the Mind which is upright in desire, and truthful in knowledge, is not disheartened at the loss of wealth : as the text asserts at the end of that part. And by this the text intends to prove that riches are as a river flowing in the distance past the upright tower of Reason, or rather of Nobility ; and that these riches cannot take Nobility away from him who has it. And in this manner in the present Song it is argued against riches.

CHAPTER XIV.

HAVING confuted the error of other men in that part wherein it was advanced in support of riches, it remains now to confute it in that part where Time is said to be a cause of Nobility, saying, "Descent of wealth ;" and this reproof or confutation is made in that part which begins : "They will not have the vile Turn noble." And in the first place one confutes this by means of an argument taken from those men themselves who err in this way ; then, to their greater confusion, this their argument is also destroyed ; and it does this when it says, "It follows then from this." Finally it concludes, their error being evident, and it being therefore time to attend to the Truth : and it does this when it says, "Sound intellct reproves."

I say, then, "They will not have the vile Turn noble." Where it is to be known that the opinion of these erroneous persons is, that a man who is a peasant in the first place can never possibly be called a Nobleman; and the man who is the son of a peasant in like manner can never be Noble; and this breaks or destroys their own argument when they say that Time is requisite to Nobility, adding that word "descent." For it is impossible by process of Time to come to the generation of Nobility in this way of theirs, which declares it to be impossible for the humble peasant to become Noble by any work that he may do, or through any accident; and declares the mutation of a peasant father into a Noble son to be impossible. For if the son of the peasant is also a peasant, and his son again is also a peasant, and so always, it will never be possible to discover the place where Nobility can begin to be established by process of Time.

And if the adversary, wishing to defend himself, should say that Nobility will begin at that period of Time when the low estate of the ancestors will be forgotten, I reply that this goes against themselves, for even of necessity there will be a transmutation of peasant into Noble, from one man into another, or from father to son, which is against that which they propound.

And if the adversary should defend himself pertinaciously, saying that indeed they do desire that it should be possible for this transmutation to take place when the low estate of the ancestors passes into oblivion, although the text takes no notice of this, it is right that the Commentary should reply to it. And therefore I reply thus: that from this which they say there follow four very great difficulties, so that it cannot possibly be a good argument. One is, that in proportion as Human Nature might become better, the slower would be the generation of Nobility, which is a very great inconvenience; since in proportion as a thing is honoured for its excellence, so much the more is it the cause of goodness; and Nobility is reckoned amongst the good. What this means is shown thus: If Nobility, which I understand as a good thing, should be generated by oblivion, Nobility would be generated in proportion to the speediness with which men might be forgotten, for so much the sooner would oblivion descend upon all. Hence, in proportion as men might be forgotten, so much the sooner would they be Noble; and, on the contrary, in proportion to the length of time during which they were held in remembrance, so much the longer it would be before they could be ennobled.

The second difficulty is, that in nothing apart from men would it be possible to make this distinction, that is to say, Noble or Vile, which is very inconvenient; since, in each species of things we see the image of Nobility or of Baseness, wherefore we often call one horse noble and one vile; and one falcon noble and one vile; and one pearl noble and one vile. And that it would not be possible to make this distinction is thus proved; if the oblivion of the humble ancestors is the cause of Nobility, or rather the baseness of the ancestors never was, it is not possible for oblivion of them to be, since oblivion is a destruction of remembrance, and in those other animals, and in plants, and in minerals, lowness and loftiness are not observed, since in one they are natural or innate and in an equal state, and Nobility cannot possibly be in their generation, and likewise neither can vileness nor baseness; since one regards the one and the other as habit and privation, which are possible to occur in the same subject; and therefore in them it would not be possible for a distinction to exist between the one and the other.

And if the adversary should wish to say, that in other things Nobility is represented by the goodness of the thing, but in a man it is understood because there is no remembrance of his humble or base condition, one would wish to reply not with words, but with the sword, to such bestiality as it would be to give to other things goodness as a cause for Nobility, and to found the Nobility of men upon forgetfulness or oblivion as a first cause.

The third difficulty is, that often the person or thing generated would come before the generator, which is quite impossible; and it is possible to prove this thus: Let us suppose that Gherardo da Cammino might have been the grandson of the most vile peasant who ever drank of the Sile or of the Cagnano, and that oblivion had not yet overtaken his grandfather; who will be bold enough to say that Gherardo da Cammino was a vile man? and who will not agree with me in saying that he was Noble? Certainly no one, however presumptuous he may wish to be, for he was so, and his memory will always be treasured. If oblivion had not yet overtaken his ancestor, as is proposed in opposition, so that he might be great through Nobility, and the Nobility in him might be seen so clearly, even as one does see it, then it would have been first in him before the founder of his Nobility could have existed; and this is impossible in the extreme.

The fourth difficulty is, that such a man, the supposed grandfather, would have been held Noble after he was dead who was not Noble whilst alive; and a more inconvenient thing could not be. One proves it thus: Let us suppose that in the age of Dardanus there might be a remembrance of his low ancestors, and let us suppose that in the age of Laomedon this memory might have passed away, and that oblivion had overtaken it. According to the adverse opinion, Laomedon was Noble and Dardanus was vile, each in his lifetime. We, to whom the remembrance of the ancestors of Dardanus has not come, shall we say that Dardanus living was vile, and dead a Noble? And is not this contrary to the legend which says that Dardanus was the son of Jupiter (for such is the fable, which one ought not to regard whilst disputing philosophically); and yet if the adversary might wish to find support in the fable, certainly that which the fable veils destroys his arguments. And thus it is proved that the argument, which asserted that oblivion is the cause of Nobility, is false.

CHAPTER XV.

SINCE, by their own argument, the Song has confuted them, and proved that Time is not requisite to Nobility, it proceeds immediately to confound their premisses, since of their false arguments no rust remains in the mind which is disposed towards Truth; and this it does when it says, "It follows then from this." Where it is to be known that if it is not possible for a peasant to become a Noble, or for a Noble son to be born of a humble father, as is advanced in their opinion, of two difficulties one must follow.

The first is, that there can be no Nobility; the other is, that the World may have been always full of men, so that from one alone the Human Race cannot be descended; and this it is possible to prove.

If Nobility is not generated afresh, and it has been stated many times that such is the basis of their opinion, the peasant man not being able to beget it in himself, or the humble father to pass it on to his son, the man always is the same as he was born; and such as the father was born, so is the son born; and so this process from one condition onwards is reached even by the first parent; for such as was the first father, that is, Adam, so must the whole Human Race be, because from him to the modern nations it will not be possible to find, according to that argument, any change whatever. Then, if Adam himself was Noble, we are all Noble; if he was vile, we are all vile or base; which is no other than to remove the distinction between these conditions, and thus it is to remove the conditions.

And the Song states this, which follows from what is advanced, saying, "That all are high or base." And if this is not so, then any nation is to be called Noble, and any is to be called vile, of necessity. Transmutation from vileness into Nobility being thus taken away, the Human Race must be descended from different ancestors, that is, some from Nobles and some from vile persons, and so the Song says, "Or that in Time there never was Beginning to our race," that is to say, one beginning; it does not say beginnings. And this is most false according to the Philosopher, according to our Faith, which cannot lie, according to the Law and ancient belief of the Gentiles. For although the Philosopher does not assert the succession from one first man, yet he would have one essential being to be in all men, which cannot possibly have different origins. And Plato would have that all men depend upon one idea alone, and not on more or many, which is to give them only one beginning. And undoubtedly Aristotle would laugh very loudly if he heard of two species to be made out of the Human Race, as of horses and asses; and (may Aristotle forgive me) one might call those men asses who think in this way. For according to our Faith (which is to be preserved in its entirety) it is most false, as Solomon makes evident where he draws a distinction between men and the brute animals, for he calls men "all the sons of Adam," and this he does when he says: "Who knows if the spirits of the sons of Adam mount upwards, and if those of the beasts go downwards?" And that it is false according to the Gentiles, let the testimony of Ovid in the first chapter of his Metamorphoses prove, where he treats of the constitution of the World according to the Pagan belief, or rather belief of the Gentiles, saying: "Man is born"—he did not say "Men;" he said, "Man is born," or rather, "that the Artificer of all things made him from Divine seed, or that the new earth, but lately parted from the noble ether, retained seeds of the kindred Heaven, which, mingled with the water of the river, formed the son of Japhet into an image of the Gods, who govern all." Where evidently he asserts the first man to have been one alone; and therefore the Song says, "But that I cannot hold," that is, to the opinion that man had not one beginning; and the Song subjoins, "Nor yet if Christians they." And it says Christians, not Philosophers, or rather Gentiles, whose opinion also is adverse, because the Christian opinion is of greater force, and is the destroyer of all calumny, thanks to the supreme light of Heaven, which illuminates it.

Then when I say, "Sound intellect reproves their words As false, and turns away," I conclude this error to be confuted, and I say that it is time to open the eyes to the Truth ; and this is expressed when I say, "And now I seek to tell, As it appears to me." It is now evident to sound minds that the words of those men are vain, that is, without a crumb or particle of Truth ; and I say sound not without cause. Our intellect may be said to be sound or unsound. And I say intellect for the noble part of our Soul, which it is possible to designate by the common word "Mind." It may be called sound or healthy, when it is not obstructed in its action by sickness of mind or body, which is to know what things are, as Aristotle expresses it in the third chapter on the Soul.

For, owing to the sickness of the Soul, I have seen three horrible infirmities in the minds of men.

One is caused by natural vanity, for many men are so presumptuous that they believe they know everything, and, owing to this, they assert things to be facts which are not facts. Tullius especially execrates this vice in the first chapter of the Offices, and St. Thomas in his book against the Gentiles, saying: "There are many men, so presumptuous in their conceit, who believe that they can compass all things with their intellect, deeming all that appears to them to be true, and count as false that which does not appear to them." Hence it arises that they never attain to any knowledge ; believing themselves to be sufficiently learned, they never inquire, they never listen ; they desire to be inquired of, and when a question is put, bad enough is their reply. Of those men Solomon speaks in Proverbs: " Seest thou a man that is hasty in his words? there is more hope of a fool than of him."

Another infirmity of mind is caused by natural weakness or smallness, for many men are so vilely obstinate or stubborn that they cannot believe that it is possible either for them or for others to know things; and such men as these never of themselves seek knowledge, nor ever reason; for what other men say, they care not at all. And against these men Aristotle speaks in the first book of the Ethics, declaring those men to be insufficient or unsatisfactory hearers of Moral Philosophy. Those men always live, like beasts, a life of grossness, the despair of all learning.

The third infirmity of mind is caused by the levity of nature; for many men are of such light fancy that in all their arguments they go astray, and even when they make a syllogism and have concluded, from that conclusion they fly off into another, and it seems to them most subtle argument. They start not from any true beginning, and truly they see nothing true in their imagination. Of those men the Philosopher says that it is not right to trouble about them, or to have business with them, saying, in the first book of Physics, that against him who denies the first postulate it is not right to dispute. And of such men as these are many idiots, who may not know their A B C, and who would wish to dispute in Geometry, in Astrology, and in the Science of Physics.

Also through sickness or defect o body, it is possible for the Mind to be unsound or sick; even as through some primal defect at birth, as with those who are born fools, or through alteration in the brain, as with the madmen. And of this mental infirmity the Law speaks when it says: "In him who makes a Will or Testament, at the time when he makes the Will or Testament, health of mind, not health of body, is required."

But to those intellects which from sickness of mind or body are not infirm, but are free, diligent, and whole in the light of Truth, I say it must be evident that the opinion of the people, which has been stated above, is vain, that is, without any value whatever, worthless.

Afterwards the Song subjoins that I thus judge them to be false and vain; and this it does when it says, "Sound intellect reproves their words As false, and turns away." And afterwards I say that it is time to demonstrate or prove the Truth; and I say that it is now right to state what kind of thing true Nobility is, and how it is possible to know the man in whom it exists; and I speak of this where I say:

>And now I seek to tell
>As it appears to me,
>What is, whence comes, what signs attest
>A true Nobility.

CHAPTER XVI.

"THE King shall rejoice in God, and all those shall be praised who swear by him, for closed is the mouth of those who speak wicked things." These words I can here propound in all truth; because each true King ought especially to love the Truth. Wherefore it is written in the Book of Wisdom,

"Love the Light of Wisdom, you, who stand before, the people," and the Light of Wisdom is this same Truth. I say, then, every King shall rejoice that the most false and most injurious opinion of the wicked and deceitful men who have up to this time spoken iniquitously of Nobility is confuted.

It is now requisite to proceed to the discussion of the Truth according to the division made above, in the third chapter of the present treatise. This second part, then, which begins, "I say that from one root Each Virtue firstly springs," intends to describe this Nobility according to the Truth, and this part is divided into two: for in the first the intention is to prove what this Nobility is; and in the second how it is possible to recognize him in whom it dwells, and this second part begins, "Such virtue shows its good." The first part, again, has two parts; for in the first certain things are sought for which are needful in order to perceive the definition of Nobility; in the second, one looks for its definition, and this second part begins, "Where virtue is, there is A Nobleman."

That we may enter perfectly into the treatise, two things are to be considered in the first place. The one is, what is meant by this word Nobility, taken alone, in its simple meaning; the other is, in what path it is needful to walk in order to search out the before-named definition. I say, then, that, if we will pay attention to the common use of speech, by this word Nobility is understood the perfection of its own nature in each thing; wherefore it is predicated not only of the man, but also of all things; for the man calls a stone noble, a plant or tree noble, a horse noble, a falcon noble, whatever is seen to be perfect in its nature. And therefore Solomon says in Ecclesiastes, "Blessed is the land whose King is Noble;" which is no other than saying, whose King is perfect according to the perfection of the mind and body; and he thus makes this evident by that which he says previously, when he writes, "Woe unto the land whose King is a child." For that is not a perfect man, and a man is a child, if not by age, yet by his disordered manners and by the evil or defect of his life, as the Philosopher teaches in the first book of the Ethics.

There are some foolish people who believe that by this word Noble is meant that which is to be named and known by many men; and they say that it comes from a verb which stands for *to know*, that is, *nosco*. But this is most false, for, if this could be, those things which were most named and best known in their species would in their species be the most noble. Thus the obelisk of St. Peter would be the most noble stone in the world; and Asdente, the shoemaker of Parma, would be more Noble than any one of his fellow-citizens; and Albuino della Scala would be more Noble than Guido da Castello di Reggio. Each one of those things is most false, and therefore it is most false that *nobile* (noble) can come from *cognoscere*, to know. It comes from *non vile* (not vile); wherefore *nobile* (noble) is as it were *non vile* (not vile).

This perfection the Philosopher means in the seventh chapter of Physics, when he says: "Each thing is especially perfect when it touches and joins its own proper or relative virtue; and then it is especially perfect according to its nature. It is, then, possible to call the circle perfect when it is truly a circle, that is, when it is joined with its own proper or relative virtue, it is then complete in its nature, and it may then be called a noble circle." This is when there is a point in it which is equally distant from the circumference. That circle which has the figure of an egg loses its virtue and it is not Noble, nor that circle which has the form of an almost full moon, because in that its nature is not perfect. And thus evidently it is possible to see that commonly, or in a general sense, this word Nobility, expresses in all things perfection of their nature, and this is that for which one seeks primarily in order to enter more clearly into the discussion of that part which it is intended to explain.

Secondly, it remains to be seen how one must proceed in order to find the definition of Human Nobility to which the present argument leads. I say, then, that since in those things which are of one species, as are all men, it is not possible by essential first principles to define their highest perfection, it is necessary to know and to define that by their effects. Therefore one reads in the Gospel of St. Matthew, when Christ speaks, "Beware of false prophets: by their fruits ye shall know them." And in a direct way the definition we seek is to be seen by the fruits, which are the moral and intellectual virtues of which this Nobility is the seed, as in its definition will be fully evident.

And these are those two things we must see before one can proceed to the others, as is said in the previous part of this chapter.

CHAPTER XVII.

SINCE those two things which it seemed needful to understand before the text could be proceeded with have been seen and understood, it now remains to proceed with the text and to explain it, and the text then begins:

> I say that from one root
> Each Virtue firstly springs,
> Virtue, I mean, that Happiness
> To man, by action, brings.

And I subjoin:

> This, as the Ethics teach,
> Is habit of right choice;

placing the whole definition of the Moral Virtues as it is defined by the Philosopher in the second book of Ethics, in which two things principally are understood. One is, that each Virtue comes from one first principle or original cause; the other is, that by "Each Virtue" I mean the Moral Virtues, and this is evident from the words, "This, as the Ethics teach."

Hence it is to be known that our most right and proper fruits are the Moral Virtues, since on every side they are in our power; and these are differently distinguished and enumerated by different philosophers. But it seems to me right to omit the opinion of other men in that part where the divine opinion of Aristotle is stated by word of mouth; and therefore, wishing to describe what those Moral Virtues are, I will pass on, briefly discoursing of them according to his opinion.

There are eleven Virtues named by the said Philosopher. The first is called Courage, which is sword and bridle to moderate our boldness and timidity in things which are the ruin of our life. The second is Temperance, which is the law and bridle of our gluttony and of our undue abstinence in those things requisite for the preservation of our life. The third is Liberality, which is the moderator of our giving and of our receiving things temporal. The fourth is Magnificence, which is the moderator of great expenditures, making and supporting those within certain limits. The fifth is Magnanimity, which is the moderator and acquirer of great honours and fame. The sixth is the Love of Honour, which is the moderator and regulator to us of the honours of this World. The seventh is Mildness, which moderates our anger and our excessive or undue patience against our external misfortunes. The eighth is Affability, which makes us live on good terms with other men. The ninth is called Truth, which makes us moderate in boasting ourselves over and above what we are, and in depreciating ourselves below what we are in our speech. The tenth is called Eutrapelia, pleasantness of intercourse, which makes us moderate in joys or pleasures, causing us to use them in due measure. The eleventh is Justice, which teaches us to love and to act with uprightness in all things.

And each of these Virtues has two collateral enemies, that is to say, vices; one in excess and one in defect. And these Moral Virtues are the centres or middle stations between them, and those Virtues all spring from one root or principle, that is to say, from the habit of our own good choice. Wherefore, in a general sense, it is possible to say of all, that they are a habit of choice standing firm in due moderation; and these are those which make a man happy in their active operation, as the Philosopher says in the first book of the Ethics when he defines Happiness, saying that Happiness is virtuous action in a perfect life.

By many, Prudence, that is, good, judgment or wisdom, is well asserted to be a Moral Virtue. But Aristotle numbers that amongst the Intellectual Virtues, although it is the guide of the moral, and points out the way by which they are formed, and without it they could not be. Verily, it is to be known that we can have in this life two happinesses or felicities by following two different roads, both good and excellent, which lead us to them: the one is the Active Life and the other is the Contemplative Life, which (although by the Active Life one may attain, as has been said, to a good state of Happiness) leads us to supreme Happiness, even as the Philosopher proves in the tenth book of the Ethics; and Christ affirms it with His own Lips in the Gospel of Luke, speaking to Martha, when replying to her: "Martha, Martha, thou art anxious and troubled about many things: verily, one thing alone is needful," meaning, that which thou hast in hand; and He adds: "Mary has chosen the better part, which shall not be taken away from her." And Mary, according to that which is previously written in the Gospel, sitting at the feet of Christ, showed no care for the service of the house, but listened only to the words of the Saviour.

For if we will explain this in the moral sense, our Lord wished to show thereby that the Contemplative Life was supremely good, although the Active Life might be good; this is evident to him who will give his mind to the words of the Gospel.

It would be possible, however, for any one to say, in argument against me: Since the happiness of the Contemplative Life is more excellent than that of the Active Life, and both may be, and are, the fruit and end of Nobility, why not rather have proceeded in the argument along the line of the Intellectual Virtues than of the Moral? To this it is possible to reply briefly, that in all instruction it is desirable to have regard to the capability of the learner, and to lead him by that path which is easiest to him. Wherefore, since the Moral Virtues appear to be, and are, more general and more required than the others, and are more seen in outward appearances, it was more convenient and more useful to proceed along that path than by the other; for thus indeed we shall attain to the knowledge of the bees by arguing of profit from the wax, as well as by arguing of profit from the honey, for both the one and the other proceed from them.

CHAPTER XVIII.

IN the preceding chapter has been determined how each Moral Virtue comes from one root, or first principle, that is, a good habit of choice; and the present text bears upon that, until the part which begins: "Nobility by right." In this part, then, it proceeds, by a way that is allowable, to teach that each Virtue mentioned above, taken singly, or otherwise generally, proceeds from Nobility as an effect from its cause, and it is founded upon a philosophical proposition, which says that, when two things are found to meet in one, both these things must be reduced to a third, or one to the other, as an effect to a cause: because one thing having stood first and of itself, it cannot exist except it be from one; and if those two could not be both the effect of a third, or else one the effect of the other, each would have had a separate first cause, which is impossible. It says, then, that

> Such virtue shows its good
>   To others' intellect,
> For when two things agree in one,
>   Producing one effect,
>
> One must from other come,
>   Or each one from a third,
> If each be as each, and more, then one
>   From the other is inferred.

Where it is to be known that here one does not proceed by an evident demonstration; as it would be to say that the cold is the generative principle of water, when we see the clouds; but certainly by a beautiful and suitable induction. For if there are many laudable things in us, and one is the principle or first cause of them all, reason requires each to be reduced to that first cause, which comprehends more things; and this ought more reasonably to be called the principle of those things than that which comprehends in itself less of their principle. For as the trunk of a tree, which contains or encloses all the other branches, ought to be called the first beginning and cause of those branches, and not those branches the cause of the trunk, so Nobility, which comprehends each and every Virtue (as the cause contains the effect) and many other actions or operations of ours which are praiseworthy, it ought to be held for such; that the Virtue may be reduced to it, rather than to the other third which is in us. Finally it says that the position taken (namely, that each Moral Virtue comes from one root, and that such Virtue and Nobility unite in one thing, as is stated above, and that therefore it is requisite to reduce the one to the other, or both to a third; and that if the one contains the value of the other and more, from that it proceeds rather than from the other third) may be considered as a rule established and set forth, as was before intended.

And thus ends this passage and this present part.

CHAPTER XIX.

SINCE in the preceding part are discussed three certain definite things which were necessary to be seen before we define, if possible, this good thing of which we speak, it is right to proceed to the following part, which begins: "Where Virtue is, there is A Nobleman." And it is desirable to reduce this into two parts. In the first a certain thing is proved, which before has been touched upon and left unproved; in the second, concluding, the definition sought is found; and this second part begins: "Comes virtue from what's noble, as From black comes violet."

In evidence of the first part, it is to be recalled to mind that it says previously that, if Nobility is worth more and extends farther than Virtue, Virtue rather will proceed from it, which this part now proves, namely, that Nobility extends farther, and produces a copy of Heaven, saying that wherever there is

Virtue there is Nobility. And here it is to be known that (as it is written in the Books of the Law, and is held as a Rule of the Law) in those things which of themselves are evident there is no need of proof; and nothing is more evident than that Nobility exists wherever there is Virtue, and each thing, commonly speaking, that we see perfect according to its nature is worthy to be called Noble. It says then: "So likewise that is Heaven Wherein a star is hung, But Heaven may be starless." So there is Nobility wherever there is Virtue, and not Virtue wherever there is Nobility. And with a beautiful and suitable example; for truly it is a Heaven in which many and various stars shine. In this Nobility there shine the Moral and the Intellectual Virtues: there shine in it the good dispositions bestowed by nature, piety, and religion; the praiseworthy passions, as Modesty and Mercy and many others; there shine in it the good gifts of the body, that is to say, beauty, strength, and almost perpetual health; and so many are the stars which stud its Heaven that certainly it is not to be wondered at if they produce many and divers effects in Human Nobility; such are the natures and the powers of those stars, assembled and contained within one simple substance, through the medium of which stars, as through different branches, it bears fruit in various ways. Certainly, with all earnestness, I make bold to say that Human Nobility, so far as many of its fruits are considered, excels that of the Angel, although the Angelic may be more Divine in its unity.

Of this Nobility of ours, which fructifies into such fruits and so numerous, the Psalmist had perception when he composed that Psalm which begins: "O

Lord our God, how admirable is Thy Name through all the Earth!" where he praises man, as if wondering at the Divine affection for this Human Creature, saying: "What is man, that Thou, God, dost visit him? Thou hast made him a little lower than the Angels; Thou hast crowned him with glory and honour, and placed him over the works of Thy hands." Then, truly, it was a beautiful and suitable comparison to compare Heaven with Human Nobility.

Then, when the Song says, "In women and the young A modesty is seen, Not virtue, noble yet," it proves that Nobility extends into parts where Virtue is not; and it says, "noble yet," alluding to Nobility as indeed a true safeguard, being where there is shame or modesty, that is to say, fear of dishonour, as it is in maidens and youths, where shame or modesty is good and praiseworthy; which shame or modesty is not virtue, but a certain good passion. And it says, "In women and the young," that is to say, in youths; because, as the Philosopher expresses it in the fourth book of the Ethics, shame, bashfulness, modesty, is not praiseworthy nor good in the old nor in men of studious habits, because to them it is fit that they beware of those things which would lead them to shame. In youths and maidens such caution is not so much required, and therefore in them the fear of receiving dishonour through some fault is praiseworthy. It springs from Nobility, and it is possible to account their timid bashfulness to be Nobility. Baseness and ignoble ways produce impudence: wherefore it is a good and excellent sign of Nobility in children and persons of tender years when, after some fault, their shame is painted in their face, which blush of shame is then the fruit of true Nobility.

CHAPTER XX.

When it proceeds to say, "Comes virtue from what's noble, as From black comes violet," the text advances to the desired definition of Nobility, by which one may see what this Nobility is of which so many people speak erroneously. It says then, drawing a conclusion from that which has been said before, that each Virtue, or rather its generator, that is to say, the habit of right choice, which stands firm in due moderation, will spring forth from this, that is, Nobility. And it gives an example in the colours, saying, as from the black the violet, so this Virtue springs from Nobility. The violet is a mixed colour of purple and black, but the black prevails, and the colour is named from it. And thus the Virtue is a mixed thing of Nobility and Passion; but, because Nobility prevails, the Virtue takes its name from it, and is called Goodness. Then afterwards it argues, by that which has been said, that no man ought to say boastfully, "I am of such and such a race or family;" nor ought he to believe that he is of this Nobility unless the fruits of it are in him. And immediately it renders a reason, saying that those who have this Grace, that is to say, this Divine thing, are almost Gods as it were, without spot of vice, and no one has the power to bestow this except God alone, with whom there is no respect of persons, even as Divine Scripture makes manifest. And it does not appear too extravagant when it says, "They are as Gods," for as it is argued previously in the seventh chapter of the third treatise, even as there are men most vile and bestial so are men most Noble and Divine. And this Aristotle proves in the seventh chapter of Ethics by the text of Homer the poet; therefore, let not those men who are of the Uberti of Florence, nor those of the Visconti of Milan, say, "Because I am of such a family or race, I am Noble," for the Divine seed falls not into a race of men, that is, into a family; but it falls into individual persons, and, as will be proved below, the family does not make individual persons Noble, but the individual persons make the family Noble.

Then when it says, "God only gives it to the Soul," the argument is of the susceptive, that is, of the subject whereon this Divine gift descends, which is indeed a Divine gift, according to the word of the Apostle: "Every good gift and every perfect gift comes from above, proceeding from the Father of Light." It says then that God alone imparts this Grace to the Soul that He sees pure, within the Soul of that man whom He sees to be perfectly prepared and fit to receive in his own proper person this Divine action; for, according as the Philosopher says in the second chapter Of the Soul, things must be prepared for their agents and qualified to receive their acts; wherefore if the Soul is imperfectly prepared, it is not qualified to receive this blessed and Divine infusion, even as a precious stone, if it is badly cut or prepared, wherever it is imperfect, cannot receive the celestial virtue; even as that noble Guido Guinizzelli said, in a Song of his which begins: "To gentle hearts Love ever will repair." It is possible for the Soul to be unqualified through some defect of temper, or perhaps through some sinister circumstances of the time in which the person lives, and into a Soul so unhappy as this the Divine radiance never shines. And it may be said of such men as these, whose Souls are deprived of this Light, that they are as deep valleys turned towards the North, or rather subterranean caves wherein the light of the Sun never enters unless it be reflected from another part which has caught its rays.

Finally, it deduces, from that which has been previously said, that the Virtues are the fruit of Nobility, and that God places that Nobility in the Soul which has a good foundation. For to some, that is, to those who have intellect, who are but few, it is evident that human Nobility is no other than the seed of Happiness.

> That seed of Happiness
> Falls in the hearts of few,
> Planted by God within the Souls
> Spread to receive His dew;

that is to say, whose body is in every part perfectly prepared, ordered, or qualified.

For if the Virtues are the fruit of Nobility, and Happiness is pleasure or sweetness acquired through or by them, it is evident that this Nobility is the seed of Happiness, as has been said. And if one considers well, this definition comprehends all the four arguments, that is to say, the material, the formal, the efficient, and the final: material, inasmuch as it says, "to the Soul spread to receive," which is the material and subject of Nobility; formal, inasmuch as it says, "That seed;" efficient, inasmuch as it says, "Planted by God within the Soul;" final, inasmuch as it says, "of Happiness," Heaven's blessing. And thus is defined this our good gift, which descends into us in like manner from the Supreme and Spiritual Power, as virtue into a precious stone from a most noble celestial body.

CHAPTER XXI.

That we may have more perfect knowledge of Human Goodness, as it is the original cause in us of all good that can be called Nobility, it is requisite to explain clearly in this especial chapter how this Goodness descends into us.

In the first place, it comes by the Natural way, and then by the Theological way, that is to say, the Divine and Spiritual. In the first place, it is to be known that man is composed of Soul and body; but that Goodness or Nobility is of the Soul, as has been said, and is after the manner of seed from the Divine Virtue. By different philosophers it has been differently argued concerning the difference in our Souls; for Avicenna and Algazel were of opinion that Souls of themselves and from their beginning were Noble or Base. Plato and some others were of opinion that they proceeded by the stars, and were Noble more or less according to the nobility of the star. Pythagoras was of opinion that all were of one nobility, not only human Souls, but with human Souls those of the brute animals and of the trees and the forms of minerals; and he said that all the difference in the bodies is form. If each one were to defend his opinion, it might be that Truth would be seen to be in all. But since on the surface they seem somewhat distant from the Truth, one must not proceed according to those opinions, but according to the opinion of Aristotle and of the Peripatetics. And therefore I say that when the human seed falls into its receptacle, that is, into the matrix, it bears with it the virtue or power of the generative Soul, and the virtue or power of Heaven, and the virtue or power of the aliments united or bound together, that is the involution or complex nature of the seed. It matures and prepares the material for the formative power or virtue which the generating Soul bestows; and the formative power or virtue prepares the organs for the celestial virtue or power, which produces, from the power of the seed, the Soul in life; which, as soon as produced, receives from the power of the Mover of the Heaven the passive intellect or mind, which potentially brings together in itself all the universal forms according as they are in its producer, and so much the less in proportion as it is farther removed from the first Intelligence.

Let no one marvel if I speak what seems difficult to understand; for to myself it seems a miracle how it is possible even to arrive at a conclusion concerning it, and to perceive it with the intellect. It is not a thing to reveal in language, especially the language of the Vulgar Tongue; wherefore I will say, even as did the Apostle: "Oh, great is the depth of the riches of Wisdom of God: how incomprehensible are Thy judgments, and Thy ways past finding out!" And since the complex nature of the seed may be better and less good, and the disposition of the receiver of the seed may be better and less good, and the disposition of the dominant Heaven to this effect may be good and better and best, which varies in the constellations, which are continually transformed; it befalls that from the human seed and from these virtues or powers the Soul is produced more or less pure; and according to its purity there descends into it the virtue or power of the possible or passive intellect, as it is called, and as it has been spoken of. And if it happen that through the purity of the receptive Soul the intellectual power is indeed separate and absolute, free from all corporeal shadow, the Divine Goodness multiplies in it, as in a thing sufficient to receive that good gift ; and then it multiplies in the Soul of this intelligent being, according as it can receive it ; and this is that seed of Happiness of which we speak at present. And this is in harmony with the opinion of Tullius in that book on Old Age when, speaking personally of Cato, he says : " For this reason a celestial spirit descended into us from the highest habitation, having come into a place which is adverse to the Divine Nature and to Eternity." And in such a Soul as this there is its own individual power, and the intellectual power, and the Divine power ; that is to say, that influence which has been mentioned. Therefore it is written in the book On Causes : " Each Noble Soul has three operations, that is to say, the animal, the intellectual, and the Divine." And there are some men who hold such opinions that they say, if all the preceding powers were to unite in the production of a Soul in their best disposition, arrangement, order, that into that Soul would descend so much of the Deity that it would be as it were another God Incarnate ; and this is almost all that it is possible to say concerning the Natural way.

By the Theological way it is possible to say that, when the Supreme Deity, that is, God, sees His creature prepared to receive His good gift, so freely He imparts it to His creature in proportion as it is prepared or qualified to receive it. And because these gifts proceed from ineffable Love, and the Divine Love is appropriate to the Holy Spirit, therefore it is that they are called the gifts of the Holy Spirit, which, even as the Prophet Isaiah distinguishes them, are seven, namely, Wisdom, Intelligence, Counsel, Courage, Knowledge, Pity, and the Fear of God. O, good green blades, and good and wonderful the seed!

And O, admirable and benign Sower of the seed, who dost only wait for human nature to prepare the ground for Thee wherein to sow! O, blessed are those who till the land to fit it to receive such seed!

Here it is to be known that the first noble shoot which germinates from this seed that it may be fruitful, is the desire or appetite of the mind, which in Greek is called "hormen;" and if this is not well cultivated and held upright by good habits, the seed is of little worth, and it would be better if it had not been sown.

And therefore St. Augustine urges, and Aristotle also in the second book of Ethics, that man should accustom himself to do good, and to bridle in his passions, in order that this shoot which has been mentioned may grow strong through good habits, and be confirmed in its uprightness, so that it may fructify, and from its fruit may issue the sweetness of Human Happiness.

CHAPTER XXII.

It is the commandment of the Moral Philosophers that, of the good gifts whereof they have spoken, Man ought to put his thought and his anxious care into the effort to make them as useful as possible to the receiver. Wherefore I, wishing to be obedient to such a mandate, intend to render this my BANQUET [Convito] as useful as possible in each one of its parts. And because in this part it occurs to me to be able to reason somewhat concerning the sweetness of Human Happiness, I consider that there could not be a more useful discourse, especially to those who know it not; for as the Philosopher says in the first book of Ethics, and Tullius in that book Of the Ends of Good and Evil, he shoots badly at the mark who sees it not. Even thus a man can but ill advance towards this sweet joy who does not begin with a perception of it. Wherefore, since it is our final rest for which we live and labour as we can, most useful and most necessary it is to see this mark in order to aim at it the bow of this our work. And it is most essential to make it inviting to those who do not see the mark when simply pointed out. Leaving alone, then, the opinion which Epicurus the philosopher had concerning it, and that which Zeno likewise had, I intend to come summarily to the true opinion of Aristotle and of the other Peripatetics. As it is said above, of the Divine Goodness sown and infused in us, from the original cause of our production, there springs up a shoot, which the Greeks term "hormen," that is to say, the natural appetite of the soul.

And as it is with the blades of corn which, when they first shoot forth, have in the beginning one similar appearance, being in the grass-like stage, and then, by process of time, they become unlike, so this Natural appetite, which springs from the Divine Grace, in the beginning appears as it were not unlike that which comes nakedly from Nature; but with it, even as the herbage born of various grains of corn, it has the same appearance, as it were : and not only in the blades of corn, but in men and in beasts there is the same similitude. And it appears that every animal, as soon as it is born, both rational and brute beast, loves itself, and fears and flies from those things which are adverse to it, and hates them, then proceeding as has been said. And there begins a difference between them in the progress of this Natural appetite, for the one keeps to one road, and the other to another ; even as the Apostle says : "Many run to the goal, but there is but one who reaches it." Even thus these Human appetites from the beginning run through different paths, and there is one path alone which leads us to our peace ; and therefore, leaving all the others alone, it is for the treatise to follow the course of that one who begins well.

I say, then, that from the beginning a man loves himself, although indistinctly ; then comes the distinguishing of those things which to him are more or less ; to be more or less loved or hated ; and he follows after and flies from either more or less according as the right habit distinguishes, not only in the other things which he loves in a secondary manner, for he even distinguishes in himself which thing he loves principally ; and perceiving in himself divers parts, those which are the noblest in him he loves most. But, since the noblest part of man is the Mind, he loves that more than the Body ; and thus, loving himself principally, and through himself other things, and of himself loving the better part most, it is evident that he loves the Mind more than the Body or any other thing ; and the Mind it is that, naturally, more than any other thing he ought to love.

Then, if the Mind always delights in the use of

the beloved thing, which is the fruit of love, the use of that thing which is especially beloved is especially delightful: the use of our Mind is especially delightful to us, and that which is especially delightful to us becomes our Happiness and our Beatitude, beyond which there is no greater delight or pleasure, nor any equal to it, as may be seen by him who looks well at the preceding argument.

And no one ought to say that every appetite is Mind; for here one understands Mind solely as that which belongs to the Rational part, that is, the Will and the Intellect; so that if any one should wish to call Mind the appetite of the Senses, here it has no place, nor can it have any abiding; for no one doubts that the Rational appetite is more noble than the Sensual, and therefore more to be loved; and so is this of which we are now speaking.

The use of our Mind is double, that is to say, Practical and Speculative (it is Practical insomuch as it has the power of acting); both the one and the other are delightful in their use, but that of Contemplation is the most pleasing, as has been said above. The use of the Practical is to act in or through us virtuously, that is to say, honestly or uprightly, with Prudence, with Temperance, with Courage, and with Justice. The use of the Speculative is not to work or act through us, but to consider the works of God and of Nature. This and the other form our Beatitude and Supreme Happiness, which is the sweetness of the before-mentioned seed, as now clearly appears. To this often such seed does not attain, through being ill cultivated, or through its tender growing shoots being perverted. In like manner it is quite possible, by much correction and cultivation of him into whom this seed does not fall primarily, to induce it by the process of steady endeavour after goodness, so that it may attain to the power of bearing this fruit. And it is, as it were, a method of grafting the nature of another upon a different stock.

No man, therefore, can hold himself excused; for if from his natural root the man does not produce sweet fruit, it is possible for him to have it by the process of grafting; and in fact there would be as many who should be grafted as those are who, sprung from a good root, allow themselves to grow degenerate.

Of the two ways of goodness, one is more full of bliss than the other, as is the Speculative, which is the use of our noblest part without any alloy, and which, for the root, Love, as has been said, is especially to be loved as the intellect. And in this life it is not possible to have the use of this part perfectly, which is to see God, who is the Supreme Being to be comprehended by the Mind, except inasmuch as the intellect considers Him and beholds Him through His effects, His Works. And that we may seek this Beatitude as the supreme, and not the other, that is, that of the Active Life, the Gospel of St. Mark teaches us, if we will look at it well.

Mark says that Mary Magdalene, and Mary the mother of James, and Mary Salome went to find the Saviour in the Tomb, and they found Him not, but they found a youth clothed in white, who said to them: "You seek the Saviour, and I tell you that He is not here; and therefore be not affrighted, but go and tell His disciples and Peter that He goeth before you into Galilee; and there ye shall see Him, as He said unto you." By these three women may be understood the three sects of the Active Life, that is to say, the Epicureans, the Stoics, and the Peripatetics, who go to the Tomb, that is to say, to the present World, which is the receptacle of corruptible things, and seek for the Saviour, that is, Beatitude, and they find it not; but they find a youth in white garments, who, according to the testimony of Matthew, and also of the other Evangelists, was an Angel of God. And therefore Matthew said: "The Angel of the Lord descended from Heaven, and came and rolled back the stone from the door, and sat upon it. His countenance was like lightning, and his raiment white as snow." The Angel is this Nobility of ours which comes from God, as it has been said, of which our argument speaks, and says to each one of these sects, that is, to whoever seeks perfect Happiness in the Active Life, that it is not here; but go and tell the disciples and Peter, that is, tell those who seek for it and those who are gone astray like Peter, who had denied Him, that He will go before them into Galilee; meaning that the Beatitude or Happiness will go before us into Galilee, that is, into Contemplation; Galilee is as much as to say, Whiteness. Whiteness is a colour full of material light, more so than any other; and thus, Contemplation is more full of Spiritual light than any other thing which is below.

And it says, "He will go before you," but it does not say, "He will be with you," to make us understand that in our contemplation God always goes before. Nor is it ever possible to us to attain to Him here, to Him, our Supreme Bliss. And it says, "There shall ye see Him, as He said unto you;" that is to say, there you will receive of His Sweetness, that is, of the Happiness as it is promised to you here, as it is established that you may receive it.

And thus it appears that our Beatitude, this

Happiness of which we speak, first we are able to find imperfect in the Active Life, that is, in the operations of the Moral Virtues, and then almost perfect in the operations of the Intellectual Virtues; which two operations are speedy and most direct ways to lead to the Supreme Bliss, which it is not possible to have here below, even as appears by that which has been said.

CHAPTER XXIII.

SINCE the definition of Nobility is sufficiently demonstrated, and since in all its parts it has been made as explicit as possible, so that we can now see who is the Nobleman, it seems right to proceed to the part of the text which begins, "Souls whom this Grace adorns," in whom appear the signs by which it is possible to know the Noble Man.

This part is divided into two. In the first it affirms that this Nobility is resplendent, and that it shines forth manifestly during the whole life of the Noble Man; in the second it appears specifically in its glory, and this second part begins, "In Childhood they obey." With regard to the first part, it is to be known that this Divine seed, which has been previously spoken of, germinates immediately in our Soul, combining with and changing its form with each form of the Soul, according to the exigency of that power. It germinates, then, as the Vegetative, as the Sensitive, and as the Rational, and it branches out through the virtues or powers of all of them, guiding all those to their perfection, and sustaining itself in them always, even to the point when, with that part of our Soul which never dies, it returns to the highest and the most glorious Sower of the seed in Heaven; and it expresses this in that first part which has been mentioned. Then when it says, "In Childhood they obey, Are gentle, modest," it shows how we can recognize the Noble Man by the apparent signs, which are the Divine operation of this goodness. And this part is divided into four, as it is made to represent four different ages, such as Adolescence, Youth, Old Age, and Extreme Old Age. The second part begins, "Are temperate in Youth;" the third begins, "Are prudent in their Age;" the fourth begins, "The fourth part of their life." Herein is contained the purpose of this part in general, with regard to which it is desirable to know that each effect, inasmuch as it is an effect, receives the likeness of its cause in proportion as it is capable of retaining it.

Wherefore, since our life, as has been said, and also the life of every living creature here below, is caused by Heaven, Heaven is revealed in all such effects as these, not, indeed, with the complete circle, but with part of it, in them. Thus its movement must be not only with them, but beyond them, and as one arch of life retains (and I say retains, not only of men, but also of other living creatures) almost all the lives, ascending and descending, they must be, as it were, similar in appearance to the form of the arch. Returning, then, to our course of life which at present we are seeking to understand, I say that it proceeds after the manner of this arch, ascending and descending. And it is to be known that the ascent of this arch should be equal to its descent, if the material of the seed from which we spring, so complex in its nature, did not impede the law of Human

Nature. But since the humid root is of better quality more or less, and stronger to endure in one effect more than in another, being subject to the nutriment of the heat, which is our life, it happens that the arch of the life of one man is of less or of greater extent than that of another, life being shortened by a violent death or by some accidental injury; but that which is called natural by the people is that span of which it is said by the Psalmist, "Thou settest up a boundary which it is not possible to pass." And since the Master among those here living, Aristotle, had perception of this arch of which we now speak, and seems to be of opinion that our life should be no other than one ascent and one descent, therefore he says, in that chapter where he treats of Youth and of Old Age, that Youth is no other than an increase of life. Where the top of this arch may be, it is difficult to know, on account of the inequality which has been spoken of above, but for the most part I believe between the thirtieth and the fortieth year, and I believe that in the perfectly natural man it is at the thirty-fifth year. And this reason has weight with me: that our Saviour Jesus Christ was a perfect natural man, who chose to die in the thirty-fourth year of His age; for it was not suitable for the Deity to have place in the descending segment; neither is it to be believed that He would not wish to dwell in this life of ours even to the summit of it, since He had been in the lower part even from childhood. And the hour of the day of His death makes this evident, for He willed that to conform with His life; wherefore Luke says that it was about the sixth hour when He died, that is to say, the height or supreme point of the day; wherefore it is possible to comprehend by that, as it were, that at the thirty-fifth year of Christ was the height or supreme point of His age. Truly this arch is not half distinguished in the Scriptures, but if we follow the four connecting links of the differing qualities which are in our composition, to each one of which appears to be appropriated one part of our age, it is divided into four parts, and they are called the four ages. The first is Adolescence, which is appropriated to the hot and moist; the second is Youth, which is appropriated to the hot and dry; the third is Old Age, which is appropriated to the cold and dry; the fourth is Extreme Old Age, which is appropriated to the cold and moist, as Albertus Magnus writes in the fourth chapter of the Metaura. And these parts or divisions are made in a similar manner in the year—in Spring, in Summer, in Autumn, and in Winter. And it is the same in the day even to the third hour, and then even to the ninth, leaving the sixth in the middle of this part, or division, for the reason which is understood, and then even to vespers, and from vespers onwards. And therefore the Gentiles said that the chariot of the Sun had four horses; they called the first Eoo, the second Piroi, the third Eton, the fourth Phlegon, even as Ovid writes in the second book of the Metamorphoses concerning the parts or divisions of the day.

And, briefly, it is to be known that, as it has been said above in the sixth chapter of the third treatise, the Church makes use of the hours temporal in the division of the day, which hours are twelve in each day, long or short according to the amount of sunlight; and because the sixth hour, that is, the midday, is the most noble of the whole day, and has in it the most virtue, the Offices of the Church are approximated thereto in each side, that is, from the prime, and thence onwards as much as possible; and therefore the Office of prime, that is, the tertius, is said at the end of that part, and that of the third part and of the fourth is said at the beginning; and therefore, before the clock strikes in a division of the day, it is termed half-third or mid-tertius; or mid-nones, when in that division the clock has struck, and thus mid-vespers.

And, therefore, let each one know that the right and lawful nones ought always to strike or sound at the beginning of the seventh hour of the day, and let this suffice to the present digression.

CHAPTER XXIV.

RETURNING to the proposition, I say that Human Life is divided into four ages or stages. The first is called Adolescence, that is, the growth or increase of life; the second is called Youth, that is, the age which can give perfection, and for this reason one understands this Youth to be perfect, because no man can give except of that which he has; the third is called Old Age; the fourth is called Senility, Extreme Old Age, as has been said above.

Of the first no one doubts, but each wise man agrees that it lasts even to the twenty-fifth year; and up to that time our Soul waits for the increase and the embellishment of the body. While there are many and very great changes in the person, the rational part cannot possess perfectly the power of discretion; wherefore, the Civil Law wills that, previous to that age, a man cannot do certain things without a guardian of perfect age.

Of the second, which is the height of our life, the time is variously taken by many. But leaving that which philosophers and medical men write concerning it, and returning to the proper argument, we may say that, in most men in whom one can and ought to be guided by natural judgment, that age lasts for twenty years. And the reason which leads me to this conclusion is, that the height or supreme point of our arc or bow is in the thirty-fifth year; just so much as this age has of ascent, so much it ought to have of descent; and this ascent passes into descent, as it were, at the point, the centre, where one would hold the bow in the hand, at which place a slight flexion may be discerned. We are of opinion, then, that Youth is completed in the forty-fifth year.

And as Adolescence is in the twenty-five years which proceed mounting upwards to Youth: so the descent, that is, Old Age, is an equal amount of time which succeeds to Youth; and thus Old Age terminates in the seventieth year.

But because Adolescence does not begin at the beginning of life—taking it in the way which has been said—but about eight months from birth; and because our life strives to ascend, and curbs itself in the descent; because the natural heat is lessened and can do little, and the moist humour is increased, not in quantity, but in quality, so that it is less able to evaporate and be consumed; it happens that beyond Old Age there remains of our life an amount, perhaps, of about ten years, a little more or a little less; and this time of life is termed Extreme Old Age, or Senility. Wherefore we know of Plato (of whom one may well say that he was a son of Nature, both because of his perfection and because of his countenance, which caused Socrates to love him when first he saw him), that he lived eighty and one years, according to the testimony of Tullius in that book On Old Age. And I believe that if Christ had not been crucified, and if He might have lived the length of time which His life according to nature could have passed over, at eighty and one years He would have been transformed from the mortal body into the eternal.

Truly, as has been said above, these ages may be longer or shorter according to our complexion or temper and our constitution or composition; but, as they are, it seems to me that I observe this proportion in all men, as has been said, that is to say, that in such men the ages may be made longer or shorter according to the integrity of the whole term of the natural life.

Throughout all these ages this Nobility of which we speak manifests its effects in different ways in the ennobled Soul; and it is that which this part of the Song, concerning which we write at present, intends to demonstrate. Where it is to be known that our good and upright nature makes forward progress in us in the reasoning powers, as we see the nature of the plants make forward progress; and therefore it is that different manners and different deportment are to be held reasonable at one age rather than at another. The ennobled Soul proceeds in due order along a single path, employing each of its powers in its time and season, or even as they are all ordained to the final production of the perfect fruit. And Tullius is in harmony with this in his book On Old Age. And putting aside the figurative sense which Virgil holds in the Æneid concerning this different progress of the ages, and letting that be which Egidius the hermit mentions in the first part On the Government of Princes, and letting that be to which Tullius alludes in his book Of Offices, and following that alone which Reason can see of herself, I say that this first age is the door and the path through which and along which we enter into our good life. And this entrance must of necessity have certain things which the good Nature, which fails not in things necessary, gives to us; as we see that she gives to the vine the leaves for the protection of the fruit, and the little tendrils which enable it to twine round its supports, and thus bind up its weakness, so that it can sustain the weight of its fruit. Beneficent Nature gives, then, to this age four things necessary to the entrance into the City of the Good Life. The first is Obedience, the second Suavity, the third Modesty, the fourth Beauty of the Body, even as the Song says in the first section of this part. It is, then, to be known that like one who has never been in a city, who would not know how to find his way about the streets without instruction from one who is accustomed to them, even so the adolescent who enters into the Wood of Error of this life would not know how to keep to the good path if it were not pointed out to him by his elders. Neither would the instruction avail if he were not obedient to their commands, and therefore at this age obedience is necessary. Here it might be possible for some one to speak thus: Then, is that man to be called obedient who shall follow evil guidance as well as he who shall believe the good? I reply that this would not be obedience, but transgression. For if the King should issue a command in one way and the servant give forth the command in another, it would not be right to obey the servant, for that would be to disobey the King; and thus it would be transgression. And therefore Solomon says, when he intends to correct his son, and this is his first commandment: "Listen, my son, to the instruction of thy father." And then he seeks to remove him immediately from the counsel and teaching of the wicked man, saying, "My son, if sinners entice thee, consent thou not."

Wherefore, as soon as he is born, the son clings to the breast of the mother; even so soon as some light of the Mind appears in him, he ought to turn to the correction of the father, and the father to instruction. And let the father take heed that he himself does not set him an example in work or action that is contrary to the words of the correction; for naturally we see each son look more to the footprints of the paternal feet than to those of other men. And therefore the Law, which provides for this, says and commands that the life of the father should appear to his sons always honourable and upright. Thus it appears that obedience was necessary in this age; and therefore Solomon writes in the Book of Proverbs, that he who humbly and obediently sustains his just reproofs from the corrector shall be glorious. And he says "shall be," to cause men to understand that he speaks to the adolescent, who cannot be so in his present age. And if any one should reflect on me because I have said obedience is due to the father and not to other men, I say that to the father all other obedience ought to be referred; wherefore the Apostle says to the Colossians: "Sons, obey your fathers in all things, for such is the will of God." And if the father be not in this life, the son ought to refer to that which is said by the father in his last Will as a father; and if the father die intestate, the son ought to refer to him to whom the Law commits his authority; and then ought the masters and elders to be obeyed, for this appears to be a reasonable charge laid upon the son by the father, or by him who stands in the father's place.

But because this present chapter has been long, on account of the useful digressions which it contains, in another chapter other things shall be discussed.

CHAPTER XXV.

NOT only this Soul, naturally good in Adolescence, is obedient, but also gentle; which is the other thing necessary in this age to make a good entrance through the portal of Youth.

It is necessary, since we cannot have a perfect life without friends, as Aristotle expresses it in the eighth book of Ethics; and the seed of the greater number of friendships seems to be sown in the first age of life, because in it a man begins to be gracious or the contrary. Such graciousness is acquired by gentle rules of conduct, as are sweet and courteous speech, gentle service courteously rendered, and actions kindly done or performed. And therefore Solomon says to the adolescent son: "Surely God scorneth the scorners; but He giveth grace unto the lowly." And elsewhere he says: "Put away from thee a froward mouth, and perverse lips put far from thee." Wherefore it appears that, as has been said, this suavity or affability is necessary.

Likewise to this age the passion of modesty is necessary; and therefore the nature which is good and noble shows it in this age, even as the Song says. And since modesty is the clearest sign, in

Adolescence, of Nobility, because there it is especially necessary to the good foundation of our life, at which the noble nature aims, it is right to speak of it somewhat. By modesty I mean three passions or strong feelings necessary to the foundation of our good life : the one is wonder, the next is modesty, the third is shame, although the common people do not discern this distinction. And all three of these are necessary to this life, for this reason : at this age it is requisite to be reverent and desirous for knowledge ; at this age it is necessary or requisite to be self-controlled, so as not to transgress or pass beyond due bounds ; at this age it is necessary to be penitent for a fault, so as not to grow accustomed to doing wrong. And all these things the aforesaid passions or strong feelings do, which vulgarly are called shame ; for wonder is an amazement of the mind at beholding great and wonderful things, at hearing them, or feeling them in some way or other ; for, inasmuch as they appear great, they excite reverence in him who sees them ; inasmuch as they appear wonderful, they make him who perceives them desirous of knowledge concerning them. And therefore the ancient Kings in their palaces or habitations set up magnificent works in gold and in marble and works of art, in order that those who should see them should become astonished, and therefore reverent inquirers into the honourable conditions of the King. Therefore Statius, the sweet Poet, in the first part of the Theban History, says that, when Adrastus, King of the Argives, saw Polynices covered with the skin of a lion, and saw Tydeus covered with the hide of a wild boar, and recalled to mind the reply that Apollo had given concerning his daughters, he became amazed, and therefore more reverent and more desirous for knowledge. Modesty is a shrinking, a drawing-back of the mind from unseemly things, with the fear of falling into them; even as we see in virgins and in good women, and in adolescent or young men, who are so modest that not only when they are tempted to do wrong, and urged to do so, but even when some fancied joy flashes across the mind, the feeling is depicted in the face, which either grows pale with fear, or flushes rosy-red. Wherefore the before-mentioned poet, in the first book of the Thebaid already quoted, says that when Acesta the nurse of Argia and Deiphile, the daughters of King Adrastus, led them before the eyes of their holy father into the presence of the two pilgrims, that is to say, Polynices and Tydeus, the virgins grew pale and blushed rosy-red, and their eyes shunned the glance of any other person, and they kept them fixed on the paternal face alone, as if there were safety. This modesty—how many errors does it bridle in, or repress? On how many immodest questions and impure things does it impose silence! How much dishonest greed does it repress! In the chaste woman, against how many evil temptations does it rouse mistrust, not only in her, but also in him who watches over her! How many unseemly words does it restrain! for, as Tullius says in the first chapter of the Offices: "No action is unseemly which is not unseemly in the naming." And furthermore, the Modest and Noble Man never could speak in such a manner that to a woman his words would not be decent and such as she could hear. Alas, how great is the evil in every man who seeks for honour, to mention things which would be deemed evil in the mouth of any woman!

Shame is a fear of dishonour through fault committed, and from this fear there springs up a penitence for the fault, which has in itself a bitter sorrow or grief, which is a chastisement and preservative against future wrong-doing. Wherefore this same poet says, in that same part, that when Polynices was questioned by King Adrastus concerning his life, he hesitated at first through shame to speak of the crime which he had committed against his father, and also for the sins of Œdipus, his father, which appeared to remain in the shame of the son; therefore he named not his father, but his ancestors, and his country, and his mother; and therefore it does indeed appear that shame is necessary to that age. And the noble nature reveals in this age, not only obedience, gentleness, affability, and modesty, but it shows beauty and agility of body, even as the Song expresses: "To furnish Virtue's person with The graces it may need." Here it is to be known that this work of beneficent Nature is also necessary to our good life, for our Soul must work in the greater part of all its operations with a bodily organ; and then it works well when the body through all its parts is well proportioned and appointed. And when it is well proportioned and appointed, then it is beautiful throughout and in all its parts; for the due ordering or proportion of our limbs produces a pleasing impression of I know not what of wonderful harmony; and the good disposition, that is to say, the health of mind and body, throws over all a colouring sweet to behold. And thus to say that the noble nature takes heed for the graces of the body, and makes it fair and harmonious, is tantamount to saying that it prepares it and renders it fit to attain the perfection ordained for it: and those other things which have been discussed seem to be requisite to Adolescence, which the noble Mind, that is to say, the noble Nature, furnishes forth to it in the first years of life, as growth of the seed sown therein by the Divine Providence.

CHAPTER XXVI.

SINCE the first section of this part, which shows how we can recognize the Noble Man by apparent signs, is reasoned out, it is right to proceed to the second section, which begins: "Are temperate in Youth, And resolutely strong."

It says, then, that as the noble Nature in Adolescence or the Spring-time of Youth appears obedient, gentle, and modest, the beautifier of its person, so in Youth it is temperate, strong, and loving, courteous and loyal; which five things appear to be, and are, necessary to our perfection, inasmuch as we have respect unto ourselves. And with regard to this it is desirable to know that just as the noble Nature prepares in the first age, it is prepared and ordained by the care or foresight of Universal Nature, which ordains and appoints the particular Nature wherever existing, to attain its perfection.

This perfection of ours may be considered in a double sense. It is possible to consider it as it has respect to ourselves, and we ought to possess this in our Youth, which is the culminating point of our life. It is possible to consider it as it has respect to others, and since in the first place it is necessary to be perfect, and then to communicate the perfection to others, it is requisite to possess this secondary perfection after this age, that is to say, in Old Age, as will be said subsequently. Here, then, it is needful to recall to mind that which was argued in the twenty-second chapter of this treatise concerning the appetite or impulse which is born in us. This appetite or impulse never does aught else but to pursue and to flee, and whenever it pursues that which is to be pursued, and as far as is right, and flies from that which is to be fled from, and as much as is right, then is the man within the limits of his perfection. Truly, this appetite or natural impulse must have Reason for its rider; for as a horse at liberty, however noble it may be by nature, by itself without the good rider does not conduct itself well, even thus this appetite, however noble it may be, must obey Reason, which guides it with the bridle and spur, as the good knight uses the bridle when he hunts. And that bridle is termed Temperance, which marks the limit up to which it is lawful to pursue; he uses the spur in flight to turn the horse away from the place from which he would flee away; and this spur is called Courage, or rather Magnanimity, a Virtue that points out the place at which it is right to stop, and to resist evil even to mortal combat. And thus Virgil, our greatest Poet, represents Æneas as under the influence of powerful self control in that part of the Æneid wherein this age is typified, which part comprehends the fourth and the fifth and the sixth books of the Æneid. And what self-restraint was that when, having received from Dido so much pleasure, as will be spoken of in the seventh treatise, and enjoying so much delectation with her, he departed, in order to follow the upright and praiseworthy path fruitful of good works, even as it is written in the fourth book of the Æneid! What impetus was that when

Æneas had the fortitude alone with Sybilla to enter into Hades, to search for the Soul of his father Anchises, in the face of so many dangers, as it is shown in the sixth book of the Æneid. Wherefore it appears that in our Youth, in order to be in our perfection, we must be Temperate and Brave. The good disposition secures this for us, even as the Song expressly states.

Again, at this age it is necessary to its perfection to be Loving; because at this age it is requisite to look behind and before, as being midway over the arch. The youth ought to love his elders, from whom he has received his being, and his nutriment, and his instruction, so that he may not appear ungrateful. He ought to love his juniors, since, in loving them, he gives them of his good gifts, for which in after-years, when the younger friends are prospering, he may be supported and honoured by them. And the poet named above, in the fifth book before-mentioned, makes it evident that Æneas possessed this loving disposition, when he left the aged Trojans in Sicily, recommended to Acestes, and set them free from the fatigues of the voyage; and when he instructed, in the same place, Ascanius his son, with the other young men, in jousting or in feats of arms; wherefore it appears that to this age Love is necessary, even as the Song says.

Again, to this age Courtesy is necessary, for, although to every age it is right or beautiful to be possessed of courteous manners, to this age it is especially necessary, because, on the contrary, Old Age, with its gravity and its severity, cannot possess courtesy, if it has been wanting in this youthful period of life; and with Extreme Old Age it is the same in a greater degree. And that most noble poet, in the sixth book before-mentioned, proves that Æneas possessed this courtesy, when he says that Æneas, then King, in order to pay honour to the dead body of Misenus, who had been the trumpeter of Hector, and afterwards accompanied Æneas, made himself ready and took the axe to assist in cutting the logs for the fire which must burn the dead body, as was their custom. Wherefore this courtesy does indeed appear to be necessary to Youth ; and therefore the noble Soul reveals it in that age, as has been said.

Again, it is necessary to this age to be Loyal. Loyalty is to follow and to put in operation that which the Laws command, and this especially is necessary in the young man ; because the adolescent, as it has been said, on account of his minority, merits ready pardon ; the old man, on account of greater experience, ought to be just, but not a follower of the Law except inasmuch as his upright judgment and the Law are at one as it were ; and almost without any Law he ought to be able to follow the dictates of his own just mind. The young man is not able to do this, and it is sufficient that he should obey the Law, and take delight in that obedience ; even as the beforesaid poet says, in the fifth book previously mentioned, that Æneas did when he instituted the games in Sicily on the anniversary of his father's death, for what he promised for the victories he loyally gave to each victor, according to their ancient custom, which was their Law.

Wherefore, it is evident that, to this age, Loyalty, Courtesy, Love, Courage, and Temperance are necessary, even as the Song says, which at present I have reasoned out ; and therefore the noble Soul reveals them all.

CHAPTER XXVII.

THAT section which the text puts forward having been reasoned out and made sufficiently clear, showing the qualities of uprightness which the noble Soul puts into Youth, we go on to pay attention to the third part, which begins, "Are prudent in their Age," in which the Song intends to show those qualities which the noble Nature reveals and ought to possess in the third age, that is to say, Old Age. And it says that the noble Soul in Old Age is prudent, is just, is liberal and cheerful, willing to speak kindly and for the good of others, and ready to listen for the same reason, that is to say, that it is affable. And truly these four Virtues are most suitable to this age. And, in order to perceive this, it is to be known that, as Tullius says in his book On Old Age, "Our life has a certain course, and one simple path, that of natural moral goodness; and to each part of our age there is given a season for certain things." Wherefore, as to Adolescence is given, as has been said above, that by means of which it may attain perfection and maturity, so to youth is given perfection and maturity in order that the sweetness of its perfect fruit may be profitable to the man himself and to others; for, as Aristotle says, man is a civil or polite animal, because it is required of him to be useful, not only to himself, but to others as well. Wherefore one reads of Cato, that he believed himself to be born not only to himself, but to his country and to all the world. Then after our own perfection, which is acquired in Youth, there must follow that which may give light not only to one's self, but to others as well; and a man ought to open and broaden like a rose as it were, which can no longer remain closed, and spread abroad the sweet odour which is bred within; and this ought to be the case in that third age which we have now in hand.

Then it must be Prudent, that is to say, Wise. And, in order to be this, a good memory of the things which have been seen is requisite, and a good knowledge of present things, and good foresight for things of the future. And, as the Philosopher says in the sixth book of Ethics, it is impossible for the man who is not good to be wise; and therefore he is not to be called a wise man who acts with cunning and with deception, but he is to be called an astute man. As no one would call him a wise man who might indeed know how to draw with the point of a knife in the pupil of the eye, even so he is not to be called a wise man who knows how to do a bad thing well, in the doing of which he must always first injure some other person. If we consider well, good counsel springs from Prudence, which leads or guides a man, and other men, to a good end in human affairs. And this is that gift which Solomon, perceiving himself to be placed as ruler over the people, asked of God, even as it is written in the Third Book of Kings; nor does the prudent man wait for counsel to be asked of him; but of himself, foreseeing the need for it, unasked he gives counsel or advice; like the rose, which not only to him who goes to her for her sweet odour freely gives it, but also to any one who passes near.

Here it would be possible for any doctor or lawyer to say: Then shall I carry my counsel or advice, and shall I give it even before it be asked of me, and shall I not reap fruit from my art or skill? I reply in the words of our Saviour: "Freely ye have received, freely give." I say, then, Master Lawyer, that those counsels which have no respect to thine art, and which proceed alone from that good sense or wisdom which God gave thee (which is the prudence of which we speak), thou oughtest not to sell to the sons or children of Him who has given it to thee. But those counsels which belong to the art which thou hast purchased, thou mayst sell; but not in such a way but that at any time the tenth part of them may be fitly set apart and given unto God, that is, to those unhappy ones to whom the Divine protection is all that is left.

Likewise at this age it is right to be Just, in order that the judgments and the authority of the man may be a light and a law to other men. And because this particular Virtue, that is to say, Justice, was seen by the ancient philosophers to appear perfect in men of this age, they entrusted the government of the cities to those men who had attained that age; and therefore the college of Rectors was called the Senate. Oh, my unhappy, unhappy country! how my heart is wrung with pity for thee whenever I read, whenever I write, anything which may have reference to Civil Government! But since in the last treatise of this book Justice will be discussed, to the present let this slight notice of it suffice.

Also at this age a man ought to be liberal, because a thing is then most suitable when it gives most satisfaction to the due requirements of its nature: nor to the due requirements of Liberality is it ever possible to give more satisfaction than at this age. For if we will look well at the argument of Aristotle in the fourth book of Ethics, and at that of Tullius in his book Of Offices, Liberality desires to be seasonable in place and time; so that the liberal man may not injure himself nor other men; which thing it is not possible to have without Prudence and without Justice, Virtues that previous to this age it is impossible to have or possess in perfection in the Natural way.

Alas! ye base-born ones, born under evil stars, ye who rob the widows and orphans, who ravish or despoil those who possess least, who steal from and occupy or usurp the homes of other men, and with that spoil you furnish forth feasts, women, horses, arms, robes, money; you wear wonderful garments, you build marvellous palaces; and you believe that you do deeds of great liberality: and this is no other than to take the cloth from the altar and to cover therewith the thief and his table! Not otherwise one ought to laugh, O tyrants, at your bounteous liberality than at the thief who should lead the invited guests into his house to his feast, and place upon his table the cloth stolen from the altar, with the ecclesiastical signs inwoven, and should not believe that other men might perceive the sacrilege. Hear, O ye obstinate men, what Tullius says against you in the book Of Offices: "Certainly there are many, desirous of being great and glorious, who rob some that they may give to others, believing themselves to be esteemed good men if they enrich their friends with what the Law allows. But this is so opposite or contrary to that which ought to be done, that nothing is more wrong."

At this age also a man ought to be Affable, to speak for the good of others, and to listen to such speech willingly, since it is good for a man to discourse kindly at an age when he is listened to. And this age also has with it a shadow of authority, for which reason it appears that the aged man is more likely to be listened to than a person in a younger period of life. And of most good and beautiful Truths it seems that a man ought to have knowledge after the long experience of life. Wherefore Tullius says, in that book On Old Age, in the person of Cato the elder: "To me is increased the desire and the delight to remain in conversation longer than I am wont." And that all four of these things are right and proper to this age, Ovid teaches, in the seventh chapter of Metamorphoses, in that fable where he writes how Cephalus of Athens came to Æacus the King for help in the war which Athens had with the Cretans. He shows that Æacus, an old man, was prudent when, having, through pestilence caused by corruption of the air, lost almost all his people, he wisely had recourse to God, and besought of Him the restoration of the dead; and for his wisdom, which in patience possessed him and caused him to turn to God, his people were restored to him in greater number than before. He shows that he was just, when he says that Æacus was the divider and the distributor of his deserted land to his new people. He shows that Æacus was generous or liberal when he said to Cephalus, after his request for aid: "O Athens! ask me not to render assistance, but take it yourself; doubt not the strength of the forces which this island possesses, nor the power of my state and realm; troops are not wanting to us, nay, we have them in excess for offence and defence; it is indeed a happy time to give you aid, and without excuse."

Alas, how many things are to be observed in this reply! but to a good, intelligent man it is sufficient for it to be placed here, even as Ovid puts it. He shows that Æacus was affable when he described, in a long speech to Cephalus, the history of the pestilence which destroyed his people, and the restoration of the same, which he tells readily.

It is clear enough, then, that to this age four things are suitable, because the noble Nature reveals them in it, even as the Song says. And that the example given may be the more memorable, Æacus says that he was the father of Telamon and Peleus and of Phocus, from which Telamon sprang Ajax and from Peleus Achilles.

CHAPTER XXVIII.

FOLLOWING the section which has been discussed, we have now to proceed to the last, that is, to that which begins, "The fourth part of their life Weds them again to God," by which the text intends to show what the noble Soul does in the last age, that is, in Extreme Old Age, that is, Senility. And it says that it does two things: the one, that it returns to God as to that port or haven whence it departed when it issued forth to enter into the sea of this life; the other is, that it blesses the voyage which it has made, because it has been upright, straight, and good, and without the bitterness of storm and tempest.

And here it is to be known that, even as Tullius says in that book On Old Age, the natural death is, as it were, a port or haven to us after our long voyage and a place of rest. And the Virtuous Man who dies thus is like the good mariner; for, as he approaches the port or haven, he strikes his sails, and gently, with feeble steering, enters port. Even, thus we ought to strike the sails of our worldly affairs, and turn to God with all our heart and mind, so that one may come into that haven with all sweetness and all peace.

And in this we have from our own proper nature great instruction in gentleness, for in such a death as this there is no pain nor bitterness, but even as a ripe apple easily and without violence detaches itself from its branch, so our Soul without grief separates itself from the body wherein it has dwelt.

Aristotle, in his book On Youth and Old Age, says that the death which overtakes us in old age is without sadness. And as to him who comes from a long journey, before he enters into the gate of his city, the citizens thereof go forth to meet him, so do those citizens of the Eternal Life go forth to meet the noble Soul; and they do thus because of his good works and acts of contemplation, which were of old rendered unto God and withdrawn from worldly affairs and thoughts. Hear what Tullius says in the person of Cato the elder: "It seems to me that already I see, and I uplift myself in the greatest desire to see, your fathers, whom I loved, and not only those whom I knew myself, but also those of whom I have heard spoken." In this age, then, the noble Soul renders itself unto God, and awaits the end of this life with much desire; and to itself it seems that it goes out from the Inn to return home to the Father's mansion; to itself it seems to have reached the end of a long journey and to have reached the City; to itself it seems to have crossed the wide sea and returned into the port. O, miserable men and vile, who run into this port with sails unfurled; and there where you should find rest, are broken by the fury of the wind and wrecked in the harbour. Truly the Knight Lancelot chose not to enter it with sails unfurled, nor our most noble Italian Guido da Montefeltro. These noble Spirits indeed furled the sails after the voyage of this World, whose cares were rendered to Religion in their long old age, when they had laid down each earthly joy and labour. And it is not possible to excuse any man because of the bond of matrimony, which may hold him in his old age, from turning to Religion, even as he who adopts the habit of St. Benedict and St. Augustine and St. Francis and St. Dominic and the like mode of life, but also it is possible to turn to a good and true Religion whilst remaining in the bonds of matrimony, for God asks of us no more than the religious heart. And therefore St. Paul says to the Romans: " For he is not a Jew which is one outwardly; neither is that circumcision which is outward in the flesh. But he is a Jew which is one inwardly; and circumcision is that of the heart, in the spirit, and not in the letter; whose praise is not of men, but of God."

And the Noble Soul in this age blesses likewise the time that is past, and it may well bless it; because when Memory turns back to them, the Noble Soul remembers her upright deeds, without which it were not possible for her to come to the port whither she is hastening with such wealth nor with such gain. And the Noble Soul does like the good merchant, who, when he draws near to his port, examines his cargo, and says: "If I had not passed along such a highway as that, I should not possess this treasure, and I should not have wherewith to rejoice in my city, to which I am approaching;" and therefore he blesses the voyage he has made.

And that these two things are suitable to this age that great poet Lucan represents to us in the second book of his Pharsalia, when he says that Marcia returned to Cato, and entreated him that he would take her back in his fourth and Extreme Old Age, by which Marcia the Noble Soul is meant, and we can thus depict the symbol of it in all Truth. Marcia was a virgin, and in that state typifies Adolescence; she then espoused Cato, and in that state typifies Youth; she then bore sons, by whom are typified the Virtues which are becoming to young men, as previously described; and she departed from Cato and espoused Hortensius, by which it is typified that she quitted Youth and came to Old Age. She bore sons to this man also, by whom are typified the Virtues which befit Old Age, as previously said. Hortensius died, by which is typified the end of Old Age, and Marcia, made a widow, by which widowhood is typified Extreme Old Age, returned in the early days of her widowhood to Cato, whereby is typified the Noble Soul turning to God in the beginning of Extreme Old Age. And what earthly man was more worthy to typify God than Cato? None, of a certainty. And what does Martia say to Cato? "Whilst there was blood in me [that is to say, Youth], whilst the maternal power was in me [that is, Age, which is indeed the Mother of all other Virtues or Powers, as has been previously shown or proved], I," says Marcia, "fulfilled all thy commandments [that is to say, that the Soul stood firm in obedience to the Civil Laws]." She says: "And I took two husbands," that is to say, I have been in two fruitful periods of life. "Now," says Marcia, "that I am weary, and that I am void and empty, I return to thee, being no longer able to give happiness to the other husband;" that is to say, that the Noble Soul, knowing well that it has no longer the power to produce, that is, feeling all its members to have grown feeble, turns to God, that is, to Him who has no need of members of the body. And Marcia says, "Give me the ancient covenanted privileges of the beds; give me the name alone of the Marriage Tie;" that is to say, the Noble Soul says to God, "O my Lord, give me now repose and rest;" the Soul says, "Give me at least whatsoever I may have called Thine in a life so long." And Marcia says, "Two reasons move or urge me to say this; the one is, that they may say of me, after I am dead, that I was the wife of Cato; the other is, that it may be said after me that thou didst not drive me away, but didst espouse me heartily." By these two causes the Noble Soul is stirred and desires to depart from this life as the spouse of God, and wishes to show that God was gracious to the creature that He made. O unhappy and baseborn men! you who prefer to depart from this life under the name of Hortensius rather than of Cato!

From Cato's name a grace comes into the close of the discourse which it was fit to make touching the signs of Nobility; because in him Nobility reveals them all, through all the ages of his life.

CHAPTER XXIX.

SINCE the Song has demonstrated those signs which in each age or period of life appear in the Noble Man, and by which it is possible to know him, and without which he cannot be, even as the Sun cannot be without light or the fire without heat, the text cries aloud to the People in the concluding part of this treatise on Nobility, and it says: "How many are deceived!" They are deceived who, because they are of ancient and famous lineage, and because they are descended of excellent and Noble fathers, believe themselves to be Noble, yet have in themselves no Nobility. And here arise two questions, to which it is right to attend at the end of this treatise. It would be possible for Manfredi da Vico, who but now is called Prætor and Prefect, to say: "Whatever I may be, I recall to mind and I represent my elders, who deserved the Office of Prefecture because of their Nobility, and they merited the honour of investiture at the coronation of the Emperor, and they merited the honour of receiving the Rose of Gold from the Roman Pontiff: I ought to receive from the People honour and reverence." And this is one question. The other is, that it would be possible for the scions of the families of San Nazzaro di Pavia and of the Piscitelli of Naples to say: "If Nobility is that which has been described, that is, that it is Divine seed graciously cast into the human Soul, and the progeny, or offshoots, have, as is evident, no Soul, it would not be possible to term any of its progeny or offshoots Noble; but this is opposed to the opinion of those who assert that our race is the most Noble in these cities."

To the first question Juvenal replies in the eighth Satire, when he begins with exclaiming, as it were: "What is the use of all these honours and of this glory which remain from the past, except that they serve as a mantle or cloak to him who may wish to cover himself with them, badly as he may live; except for him who talks of his ancestors, and points out their great and wonderful works, giving his own mind to miserable and vile actions?" And this satirical poet asks: "Who will call that man Noble, because of his good race, who is not worthy of his race? It is no other than to call the Dwarf a Giant." Then afterwards he says to such an one as this: "Between thee and the statue erected in memory of thine ancestor there is no other dissimilarity except that its head is of marble and thine is alive." And in this (with reverence I say it) I disagree with the poet, for the statue of marble or of wood or of metal, which has remained in memory of some worthy brave man, differs much in effect from the wicked descendant: because the statue always confirms a good opinion in those who have heard of the good renown or fame of him whose statue it is, and it begets good opinion in others. But the wicked son or nephew does quite the contrary; he weakens the good opinion of those who have heard of the goodness of his ancestors. For some one says to himself in his thought: "It cannot possibly be true, all this that has been said about this man's ancestors, since from their seed one sees an offshoot such as that." Wherefore he ought to receive not honour, but dishonour, who bears false or evil witness against the good. And therefore Tullius says that the son of the brave man ought to strive to bear good witness to the father. Wherefore, in my judgment, even as he who defames an excellent man deserves to be shunned by all people and not listened to, even so the vile man descended from good ancestors deserves to be banned by all; and the good man ought to close his eyes in order not to see that infamous man casting infamy upon the goodness which remains in Memory alone. And let this suffice at present to the first question that was moved.

To the second question it is possible to reply that a race of itself has no Soul; and indeed it is true that it is called Noble, but it is in a certain way. Wherefore it is to be known that every whole is composed of its parts, and there is a certain whole which has a simple essence in its parts, as in one man there is one essence in all and in each individual part; and this which is said to be in the part is said in the same way to be in the whole. There is another whole which has not a common essential form or essence with the parts, as a heap of corn; but there is a secondary essence which results from many grains, which possess in themselves a true and primary essence. And in such a whole as this they are said to be the qualities of the parts in a secondary way; wherefore it is called a white heap, because the grains whereof the heap is made are white. Truly this white appearance is more in the grains in the first place, and in the second place it results in the whole heap, and thus secondarily it is possible to call it white; and in such a way it is possible to call a race Noble. Wherefore it is to be known, that as in order to make a white heap the white grains must be most numerous, so to make a Noble race the Noble Men must be more numerous than the others, so that their goodness, with its good fame or renown, may cover the opposite quality which is within. And as from a white heap of corn it would be possible to pick up the wheat grain by grain, and substitute, grain by grain, red maize, till, finally, the whole heap or mass would change colour, so would it be possible for the good men of the Noble race to die out one by one, and the wicked ones to spring up therein, who would so change the name or fame thereof, that it would have to be called, not Noble, but vile, or base.

And let this be a sufficient answer to the second question.

CHAPTER XXX.

As it has been shown previously in the third chapter of this treatise, this Song has three principal parts, whereof two have been reasoned or argued out, the first of which begins in the aforesaid chapter, and the second in the sixteenth (so that the first through thirteen, and the second through fourteen chapters, passes on to an end, without counting the Proem of the treatise on the Song, which is comprised in two chapters), in this thirtieth and last chapter we must briefly discuss the third principal part, which was made as a refrain and as a species of ornament for this Song; and it begins: "My Song, Against the strayers."

Here it is chiefly to be known that every good

workman, at the end of his work, ought to ennoble and embellish it as much as possible, that it may leave his hands so much the more precious, and more worthy of fame. And this I endeavour to do in this part, not as a good workman, but as the follower of one.

I say, then, "My Song, Against the strayers." "Against the strayers" is a phrase, as, for example, from the good friar, Thomas of Aquinas, who, to a book of his, which he wrote to the confusion of all those who go astray from our Faith, gave the title "Contra Gentili," Against the Heathen. I say, then, that thou shalt go, which is as much as to say: "Thou art now perfect, and it is now time, not to stand still, but to go forward, for thy enterprise is great. And 'when you reach Our Lady, hide not from her that your end Is labour that would lessen wrong.'" Where it is to be observed that, as our Lord says, "We ought not to cast pearls before swine," because it is not to their advantage, and it is injury to the pearls; and, as Æsop the poet says in the first fable, a little grain of corn is of far more worth to a cock than a pearl, and therefore he leaves the pearl and picks up the grain of corn: reflecting on this, as a caution, I speak and give command to the Song that it reveal its high office where this Lady, that is, where Philosophy, will be found. And that most noble Lady will be found when her dwelling-place is found, that is, the Soul in which she finds her Inn. And this Philosophy dwells not in wise men alone, but likewise, as is proved above in another treatise, wherever the love for her inhabits, she is there. "And to such as these," I say to the Song, "thou mayst reveal thine office, because to them the purpose thereof will be useful, and by them its thoughts will be gathered in."

And I bid it say to this Lady, "I travel ever talking of your Friend."

Nobility is her Friend. For so much does the one love the other, that Nobility always seeks her, and Philosophy does not turn aside her most sweet glance to any other.

O, what a great and beautiful ornament is this which is given to her in the last part of this Song, by giving to her the title of Friend, the Friend of her whose own abode is in the most secret depths of the Divine Mind.

NOTE

ON THE DATE OF THE CONVITO.

It is natural to suppose that Dante's death at Ravenna in 1321 caused the Convito, a work of his latter years, to be left unfinished. But there are arguments that have been especially dwelt upon by writers who regard the Convito as a work begun before the conception of the Divine Comedy, and dropped when the Poet's mind became intent upon that masterpiece.

One argument is that the Divine Comedy is nowhere mentioned or alluded to in the Convito. But as the place designed for the Convito is midway between the Vita Nuova, which preceded it, and the Divine Comedy, which was to follow, references to the poem which was not yet before the reader would have been a fault in art.

Another argument is drawn from the fourteenth chapter of the Second Treatise, where (on page 84 in this volume) the shadow in the Moon is ascribed to "the rarity of its body, in which the rays of the Sun can find no end wherefrom to strike back again as in the other parts." In the second canto of the Purgatorio, Beatrice opposes that opinion, whence it may be inferred that Dante had learnt better, and he speaks of this again in a later canto (the twenty-second) as a former opinion. This leads to an inference that the Second Treatise was written before 1300.

Attention is due also to a passage in the third chapter of the First Treatise (on pages 16 and 17 in this volume), in which Dante speaks of his long exile and poverty. The exile and the wanderings of Dante began after the year

1300. He was befriended by Guido da Polenta in Ravenna, by Uguccione della Faggiola in Lucca, by Malaspina in the Lunigiana, by Can Grande della Scala in Verona, by Bosone de' Raffaelli in Gubbio, by the Patriarch Pagano della Torre in Udine. In 1311, when the Emperor Henry of Luxembourg went to Italy, Dante had some hope of return, which passed away in 1313 when that Emperor died in Buonconvento. Dante remained in exile. In 1321 his patron, Guido Novello da Polenta, sent him on an embassy to Venice, in which he was unsuccessful. The sea way being blocked, he had to return by land, and he was struck by the malaria which caused his death by fever on the 14th of September in that year, 1321. This reference to long exile leads to an inference that the First Treatise was written much later than 1300.

But, again, there is a passage in the third chapter of the Fourth Treatise (on page 171 of this volume) that points to an earlier date. Frederick of Suabia is named as the Emperor who

> held,
> As far as he could see,
> Descent of wealth, and generous ways,
> To make Nobility.

Dante calls him "the last Emperor of the Romans," and adds, "I say last with respect to the present time, notwithstanding that Rudolf, and Adolphus, and Albert were elected after his death and from his descendants." This last of the Romans was that famous Frederick II., who died in 1250, and of whom Dante said in his Treatise on the Language of the People: "The illustrious heroes, Frederick Cæsar and his son Manfredi, followed after elegance and scorned what was mean; so that all the best compositions of the time came out of their Court. Thus, because their royal throne was in Sicily, all the poems of our predecessors in the Vulgar Tongue were called Sicilian." Rudolf I. of

NOTE ON THE DATE OF THE CONVITO.

Hapsburg, founder of the Imperial House of Austria, was elected Emperor in 1273, after a time of confusion and nominal rule. He died in 1291, and, instead of his son Albert, Adolphus of Nassau was next elected Emperor. But in June 1298 Albert obtained election; Adolphus was deposed, and was soon afterwards killed in battle with his rival. Albert was murdered on the 6th of May, 1308, and, after an interregnum of seven months, he was succeeded by Henry VII. of Luxembourg. Now, Dante's list does not go on from Albert to Henry. It is assumed, therefore, that this passage must have been written before the end of the year 1308.

There is another passage at the close of chapter vi. of the Fourth Treatise (on page 186 in this volume) that points to a like inference of date. Dante writes: "Ye enemies of God, look to your flanks, ye who have seized the sceptres of the kingdoms of Italy. And I say to you, Charles, and to you, Frederick, Kings, and to you, ye other Princes and Tyrants, see who sits by the side of you in council." The Charles and Frederick here addressed were Charles II. of Anjou, King of Naples, and Frederick of Aragon, King of Sicily; and King Charles died in the year 1310.

It has been inferred, therefore, that the four treatises of the Convito were not written consecutively. The Second Treatise may have been begun some time after the death of Beatrice, in 1290, time being allowed after 1290 for the completion of the Vita Nuova and a period of devotion to philosophic studies. That Second Treatise having been first written, the Treatise on Nobility, the Fourth, may have next followed; and this may have been written before the end of the year 1298. The Third Treatise may have been written later, and made to connect the Second and the Fourth. The First Treatise, or General Introduction, which has in it clear indication of a later date, may have been written last, when the whole design was brought into shape.

NOTE ON THE DATE OF THE CONVITO.

Various reasons have been used for dating this final arrangement of the plan for an Ethical survey of human knowledge in fifteen treatises, and the suggested date is the year 1314. The whole work seems to have been planned. Besides the references to the Fifteenth Treatise, there is a glance forward to the matter of the Seventh Treatise in the twenty-sixth chapter of the Fourth.

The question of date is not of great importance, and this may console us though we know that it can never be settled. Here it is only touched upon to show the significance of one or two historical allusions in the book.

www.ingramcontent.com/pod-product-compliance
Lightning Source LLC
Chambersburg PA
CBHW032116230426
43672CB00009B/1760